JOHN LONIE was resident writer/researcher with the Magpie Company at the State Theatre Company of South Australia between 1979 and 1982, after which he became Associate Director and Dramaturg at St Martins in Melbourne. He has recently spent a year as a student at the Film and Television School in Sydney and is now a freelance writer.

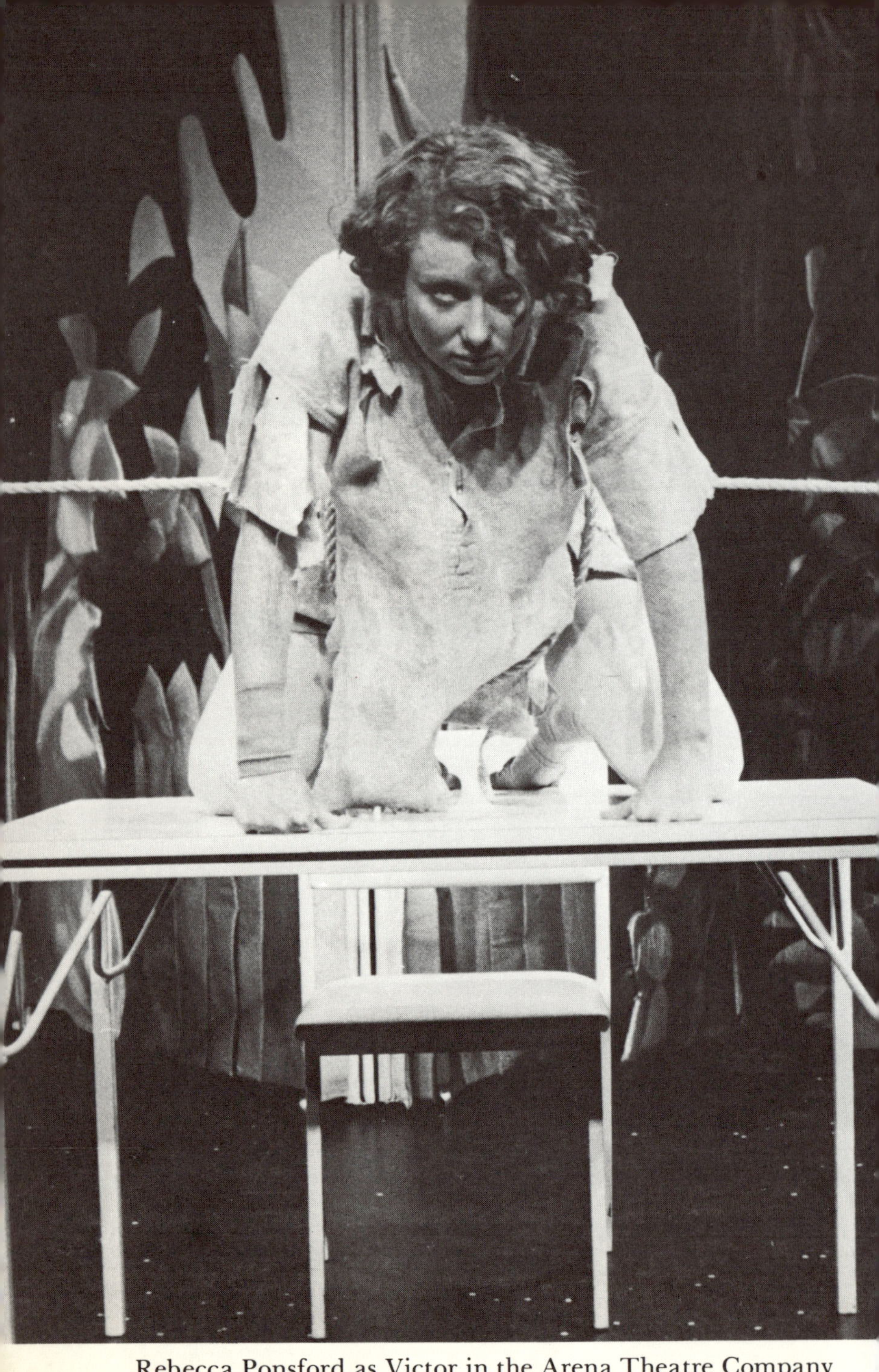

Rebecca Ponsford as Victor in the Arena Theatre Company production of *Wolf Boy* at the Sydney Festival 1985. Photo by Peter Charlton.

LEARNING FROM LIFE

Five Plays for Young People
selected and introduced by

John Lonie

CURRENCY PRESS · SYDNEY

CURRENCY PLAYS
General Editor: Katharine Brisbane

First published in 1985
by Currency Press Pty Ltd
P O Box 452, Paddington, NSW, 2021, Australia

National Library of Australia card number and ISBN 0 86819 120 5

Typeset and printed by Colorcraft Ltd, Hong Kong

Contents

Introduction

John Lonie

Over the past decade, theatre-in-education has changed the face of theatre as seen by thousands of Australian school-age children.

Most people can remember the agonies of a school Shakespeare, not least the poor actors who had to struggle against the deep resentment coming to them in waves across the footlights — resentment against the public examination, the theatre auditorium, the teachers who forced them to attend, Shakespeare and all his works, the whole English language and theatre itself! Not a happy memory. Compulsory theatre 'because it is on the syllabus' still thrives, sadly, but no longer is it the only theatre that children can see. And this happy fact is due in a large way to the visit to most schools in most States by theatre-in-education companies. Indeed, some companies when on country tour bring the only live theatre many small communities ever see.

For most children, a performance by one of the TIE companies — as they are called — will be their introduction to 'live' theatre. For example, a child in a Year Four class in Adelaide could see a play in his or her classroom in which an odd-looking Wizard appears in the nick of time to help out a 'maths offender' before he is consigned to oblivion — a play in which the didactic element is overcoming the mysteries of arithmetic. In Hobart, a class of Year Six children could see a play in which an old man recreates his adventures as a child escaping Nazi-held Austria, eventually, arriving in

Australia. In Sydney, a Year Nine group could see a play which persuades them that their teachers are pretty human, when all is said and done. One of the excellent things about TIE is that it is always portable, so that what is seen by children in Adelaide, Hobart or Sydney can also be seen by children in provincial towns of either large or 'one-horse' variety. What is special about these TIE plays is that each is tailor-made for its audience.

The plays are presented by companies made up mainly of youthful professionals, who have a special interest in this field of theatre craft and whose ideology dictates the treatment of children as autonomous individuals with a growing capacity to think things out for themselves. It is no surprise, therefore, that the various companies, along with the community-based theatres, present the most innovative theatre one can find in Australia. This is nothing but a wise strategy, because audiences untrained in bourgeois theatre manners very quickly let performers know if they are boring them or not. It is this immediacy of response which is so attractive to TIE practitioners. And it keeps them on their toes. All can recall with a squirm 'when we lost them'.

Theatre-in-education has a relatively short history and has distinctly English origins. It began in a formal sense in 1965 at the Belgrade Theatre in the English city of Coventry. As a movement, it had sprung from those involved in educational drama, and from those in theatre concerned to enlarge their audience by gearing their work to the interests of those who hardly, if ever, attended theatre. Fostering a liking for theatre among children was an obvious way to blend both the interests of theatre and of education. It was this development which soon found its way to Australia with, for example, the work of Barbara Manning and her Salamanca Theatre Company, which is still one of the country's finest. We were lucky also to attract to Australia some of the English TIE founders, such as Roger Chapman, who set up Magpie, based at the State Theatre in Adelaide; and David Young, who is presently Artistic Director at Toe Truck Theatre in Sydney, soon to take over at Salamanca.

Of course, didactic theatre has a longer history and has informed the development of theatre-in-education. Consider the work of Piscator and Brecht in Weimar Germany; the agitprop theatre in the early years of the new Soviet Republic; and the Federal Theatre Project in the United States of the New Deal, with its 'Living Newspaper' companies. In our own country, the work of the New Theatre under the aegis of the Communist Party is the best expression of this kind of theatre.

Any good play has a message for its audience. The idea that if one has a message it should be 'sent by telegram' as the Americans say, is utterly fatuous. All artists wish to communicate their ideas to others — the fiction writer through a short story or novel, the poet with a poem or the painter with a picture. The playwright chooses the medium of entertainment in its broad sense; entertainment on the stage. Those who recoil at the notion of a didactic theatre recoil from a theatre of ideas and, sadly, their number in our country is legion. As Brecht, who knew a thing or two, once wrote, '. . . theatre remains theatre even while it is didactic and as long as it is good theatre, it is also entertaining.'[1]

The belief common to all theatre-in-education is that theatre is not an end in itself. It is a means of communication in which content is vital. As most teachers would readily testify, entertainment is a marvellous vehicle for learning. And 'learning' is the operative word in theatre-in-education, for it is really a learning theatre, in which children have the opportunity to learn by direct experience in the participatory projects, or indirectly by watching the experience of others dramatised by a group of actors. It is why so many of those involved in TIE work also have teacher training. I would argue, however, that this is not absolutely necessary. The communications skills of the actor are more important. But to have both, as most actors in TIE do, is a great bonus.

The link between the companies and the teachers in the schools must be a good one, and one that works both ways. Teachers need to know what to expect and the companies need to know something about their prospective audiences. It is all very well for a company to go into a classroom and present a wonderful play about school children ganging up and despatching teacher; the company waltzes happily away to a new venue leaving the teacher to cope with the consequences. However, companies generally provide good follow-up notes and suggestions for classroom activities for teachers and their students on themes connected with the play. Many companies have schools officers who are in constant contact with the teachers.

The five plays chosen for this collection were selected primarily because each is a fine piece of theatre which has something worthwhile to say. Each has been in production and has been seen by thousands of children of all ages. They include two of the most successful and popular TIE plays produced so far in Australia — *Wolf Boy* by Peter Charlton of the Arena Theatre in Melbourne, and the Magpie play *Until Ya Say Ya Love Me*, whose subject — teenagers and sexuality — attracted overwhelming approval, with a touch of disapproval from some quarters. Together the plays represent the development of an Australian theatre-in-education, one in which the original English influence, while still evident, is less obvious than in plays of ten years ago. While it is hazardous to generalise, the Australian style of TIE has moved away from the more confrontationist and prescriptive English work to plays which are more lyrical and theatrical. This is most evident in *Wolf Boy*. The mark common to all the plays is that they are very domestic, and their political content and intent are covert rather than overt. I believe this is a recognition of the sort of society which caucasian Australians have created, one which is very domestic and, in relation to our English and other European cousins, unpolitical. Political subtlety is a necessary ingredient of Australian work not only because of our 'unpolitical' political culture, but also because of the conservative and centralised education system. It is frustrating for those among us who would prefer a more openly political and confrontationist kind of theatre. However, I believe the plays in this collection have a strong political content — one of a progressive nature.

The collection has also been designed to cover most age

groups from lower primary to the end of high school. For the collection it was important to try to represent the different ways in which theatre-in-education plays are created. *Wolf Boy* and *Wasting Away* were both written by individual writers — Peter Charlton and David Young respectively. *If Only We Had a Cat* was written by Richard Tulloch in collaboration with the Toe Truck Theatre Company of which he was then Artistic Director. Both *Until Ya Say Ya Love Me* and *Hey Mum, I Own a Factory*! are collaborative efforts from the Magpie Company of the State Theatre in Adelaide.

Behind the ripe old cliché that this is a changing world, is an idea of great hidden power, power which if realised would frighten the life out of the tsars of education. For how does the world change? Who changes it? Who benefits from those changes? These matters are the hidden agenda of any education system, yet the actual questions are almost never asked of the children the education system seeks to enlighten. To do so would be to stimulate dangerous tendencies in the children. Yet these dangerous ideas are exactly those which should be fostered by an education which seeks to equip a child with the tools to survive and thrive. They certainly inform the theory of education which is behind each of these plays. Children have a right to find out how their society changes and to learn that when they are grown-up, they can be initiators of their own histories. Knowledge is the key to understanding these changes and through the craft of theatre, knowledge is very well imparted.

These plays are unashamedly 'message' plays and for that, they are better theatre.

Sydney, December 1984

[1] Bertolt Brecht, Introductory Note: *The Measures Taken*, Eyre Methuen, London, 1977.

Ian Pidd, Josephine Lee and Peta Rutter in the Toe Truck Theatre production of *If Only We Had a Cat*. Photo by Sandy Edwards.

If Only We Had a Cat

Richard Tulloch

FOREWORD

You could see the fear in the teacher's eyes as the Toe Truck Theatre van arrived.

'I'm afraid there's been a bit of a mix up. The hall's double-booked.'

A hundred and eighty kids jostled in a queue at the door. Inside the hall bingo tables were being set up and the first busloads of senior citizens were arriving in the street.

'Couldn't we do the play somewhere else? Haven't you got a library?'

'You're joking.'

'Well, could we invite the oldies to stay and see the play?'

'What's it about?'

'Jewish refugees arriving in Australia in the 1930s.'

'Sounds like heavy stuff. They're old, you know. They just want to be entertained.'

'There's some funny bits in it too.'

So they stayed, enjoyed the play, and there was a lively discussion after the performance between those who had lived through the Depression and those who hadn't heard of it till that morning.

'Aha,' thought the director, desperately searching for a good idea for next year's programme, 'there should be more of this!'

The following year we devised *If Only We Had a Cat*, and asked schools booking the company to invite the children's grandparents to come too. Most schools took up the challenge and for some it was the start of more regular contact between the students and old people in the community.

My thanks to the teachers who organised those performances, to the staff and residents of retirement villages who helped us in our research, to Agnes Tulloch for library research, to Nici Wood who directed the original Toe Truck production and to actors Josephine Lee, Ian Pidd and Peta Rutter on whose clever improvisations most of this script is based.

Richard Tulloch, March 1985

RICHARD TULLOCH devised and directed plays for children while he was a student at Melbourne University. He later worked for ABC radio, then for the Magic Mushroom Mime Troupe before spending two years in Europe with youth and community theatre companies. He was Associate Director of the National Theatre Company in Perth before joining Toe Truck Theatre in Sydney as Artistic Director in 1980. Toe Truck represented Australia at the Theatres of the World festival in Lyon, France in 1983, performing two of his plays. His other plays include *Kaspajack* (1977), *The Cocky of Bungaree* (1978) and *Year Nine are Animals* (1981). He now works as a freelance writer, actor and director.

If Only We Had a Cat was first performed by Toe Truck Theatre, Sydney, at Chittaway Bay Public School on 24 February 1983, with the following cast:

ALICE	Josephine Lee
ALBERT STEVE DOCTOR	Ian Pidd
JULIA MATRON MARGARET	Peta Rutter

Directed by Nici Wood
Designed by Noel Howell
Music by Richard Tulloch

EDITOR'S NOTE

The Toe Truck production was also performed at retirement villages and for senior citizens groups. At school performances children were invited to bring grandparents with them to see the play.

CHARACTERS

DR ALICE STONER, botanist, 82 years old
STEVE, university student
JULIA, university student
ALBERT, Alice's neighbour
MARGARET, Albert's daughter
DOCTOR
MATRON

SETTING

The location for most of the action is ALICE's second floor room in the Renby Road Retirement Hostel. It is neat, clean and sterile. Right is a door which leads into the corridor; left another door leads into ALICE's bathroom. This door has a small vent near the bottom. Through the open window a branch of a tree can be seen, and beyond that a 'sky' screen, which can change colour to represent day or night.

IF ONLY WE HAD A CAT

SCENE ONE

Music. The three actors enter. They are dressed in neutral costume and carry tea cups and saucers. They shuffle on stage and sit in what is almost a parody of 'old age' acting. In unison they blow on their tea, stir it and drink. As they replace their teacups on the saucers one of them drops a teaspoon. The others look on in disapproval as the teaspoon is retrieved. They drink again in unison. This should bring some laughter from the audience, at which point the actors put down their cups and speak in their normal voices.

ACTOR 1: Sooner or later we all grow old.

ACTOR 2: We weren't always old.

ACTOR 3: We were all young once.

TOGETHER: Once upon a time.

    [*Actor 1 steps forward and becomes* ALICE STONER.]

ALICE: Hello. I'm Dr Alice Stoner. I'm eighty-two. I'm not a medical doctor. I'm a scientific doctor — a botanist. Do you know what botany is?

    [*She acknowledges any response from the audience.*]

That's right — it's the study of plants. I've spent all my life studying plants, collecting plants, writing about plants, reading about plants and lecturing about plants at the University.

    [*Actors 2 and 3 become* STEVE *and* JULIA, *students at a rowdy university lecture.* ALICE *is just finishing a lecture.*]

Just before you leave this class, may I remind you that your essays on cross pollination in *Eucalyptus grandis* . . .

    [STEVE *groans.*]

It's Latin for 'big gum tree', Steve. Your essays are now overdue. These essays count for marks at the end of the year. Enough said, thank you.

[*The lecture breaks up.* ALICE *starts to leave.* STEVE *and* JULIA *follow her, carrying teacups.*]

JULIA: Dr Stoner . . .

ALICE: Yes, Julia?

JULIA: I left my essay on the desk in your office.

ALICE: Thank you, Julia. Where's yours, Stevo?

STEVE: I couldn't get it finished, Dr Stoner. I've just had my appendix out.

ALICE: That's the third time this year you've had your appendix out.

STEVE: It's a really bad one, Dr Stoner. Couldn't you give me another week?

ALICE: On one condition — you give me a lift home.

STEVE: On the motorbike?

ALICE: On the motorbike.

STEVE: You're too old for that, Dr Stoner.

ALICE: I'm not too old for anything, Stevo.

STEVE: OK.

[*They sit, straddling seats as if on a motorbike.* STEVE *mimes the handlebars and makes the sound of the bike vocally.* ALICE *finds the ride a bit shaky but she will not admit to nervousness.*]

ALICE: How am I doing, Stevo?

STEVE: Pretty good.

ALICE: I could get to like this.

STEVE: You could start your own bikie gang.

ALICE: Hell's Grannies.

[*The ride ends.* ALICE *dismounts.*]

Thanks, Stevo.

STEVE: [*jokingly*] Don't get run down crossing the street!

[ALICE *waves back to him, then mimes waiting to cross the street. She steps onto the road, there is a screech of brakes and she falls to the ground. An ambulance siren is heard.* ACTOR 2 *becomes a* DOCTOR. ACTOR 3 *exits as* ALICE *is helped to a seat.*]

ALICE: Doctor . . .

DOCTOR: Listen, Alice, you've broken your hip. It will take some time for the bones to knit.

ALICE: How long?

DOCTOR: [*evasively*] It's hard to say with someone your age.
    [*He wheels in a wheelchair.*]
ALICE: [*horrified*] Will I be able to walk again?
    [*She is helped into the wheelchair. She can just walk,
    leaning heavily on the stick, but the* DOCTOR *insists on
    seating her.*]
DOCTOR: Alice, you're going to need help. You won't be
    able to get about much to do your shopping and cooking.
ALICE: You're not going to put me in a home?
DOCTOR: I suggest the Renby Road Retirement Hostel. It's
    a nice place. They look after you well there.
    [*He wheels her to centre stage and exits.*]

SCENE TWO

Music. MATRON *enters. She carries a large overnight bag
which contains clothes belonging to* ALICE. *She begins to
open up the set to reveal* ALICE's *room.*

MATRON: Here we are, Alice. This is your room. It's nice up
    here on the second floor; you get a gorgeous view of the
    garden. You're lucky to have a room on this side of the
    building, you know. It's lovely and cool during the
    summer.
ALICE: I'll be gone from here before summer.
MATRON: Sorry, dear?
ALICE: I said, I'll be gone before summer.
MATRON: Nonsense, Alice, don't be silly. You're not going
    to die. The doctor said you had nothing to worry about.
ALICE: I meant I'll be well again before summer.
MATRON: [*unconvincingly*] Yes, of course you will. Now
    your bathroom is through this door here. You have to
    share it with the person next door.
    [*She begins to unpack* ALICE's *bag.*]
ALICE: I can do that.
MATRON: Sorry, dear?
ALICE: I can unpack my own bag.

MATRON: It's no trouble, Alice, really. It's what I'm paid to do.

ALICE: But all my private things are in there!

MATRON: I'll just undo the buckle for you.

> [*She does so, and takes a large pair of silk bloomers from the case.*]

Oh, Alice, aren't they lovely!

ALICE: [*furiously*] Matron!

MATRON: Yes, dear?

ALICE: I may be eighty-two years old but I am not deaf and I am not stupid and I do not enjoy being treated like a child. Now kindly leave me alone!

MATRON: [*taken aback*] All right, dear.

> [*She starts to leave.* ALICE *raises herself out of the wheelchair with the aid of a stick.* MATRON *sees what an effort this costs her.*]

Perhaps you should have a little rest now, Alice.

> [*She gently helps* ALICE *back into the wheelchair.*]

We have dinner here at five-thirty. Do you like shepherd's pie?

> [*She exits, just as* ALICE *is about to speak.*]

ALICE: [*to herself*] Actually I *was* a vegetarian.

> [*She painfully crosses the room and starts to unpack her bag. Then she notices that the door is slowly opening. She turns around but the door shuts quickly. This happens again, so she gets to her feet and goes to hide by the door. This time when the door opens she thrusts out her stick and catches* ALBERT, *who is entering furtively.* ALBERT *is wearing a dressing gown and slippers.*]

Hello.

> [ALBERT *smiles but makes no answer.*]

Did you want something?

> [ALBERT *shakes his head.*]

I'm Alice Stoner.

> [ALBERT *nods.*]

What's your name?

ALBERT: Albert.

> [*There is an awkward pause. He takes a packet of biscuits from his pocket and puts one in his mouth.*]

I just popped in to see if you were settling in all right.

ALICE: Yes, I am, thank you, Albert.

ALBERT: [*indicating the wheelchair*] You've got a wheelchair.

ALICE: Oh, it's not mine. It belongs to the home.

ALBERT: [*seating himself in the wheelchair*] I'm not a well man.

[*He stands and starts to exit through the bathroom door.*]

I just popped in to see if you were settling in all right. My room's next door. [*Suggestively*] We share the same bathroom.

[*He winks and exits.* ALICE *waits a moment then begins a series of stretching exercises, holding her walking stick in front of her and bending from the waist while sitting in the wheelchair. The bathroom door opens furtively and* ALBERT *is there again.* ALICE *doesn't notice him at first.*]

Life. Be in it, eh?

[ALICE *stops exercising.* ALBERT *holds out a tube of toothpaste.*]

If you're ever short of toothpaste . . .

[*He puts the tube in his pocket.*]

Doing your exercises?

ALICE: It's physiotherapy, Albert, to help my hip get better.

ALBERT: Good on yer, Alice. You show 'em.

[*He sits down, which rather puts her out.*]

Don't let me interrupt.

[ALICE *is forced to continue. He offers her his packet of biscuits.*]

Like a biscuit?

ALICE: [*continuing grimly*] No thank you.

ALBERT: Quite right too. Bad for the figure, eh?

[*He puts away his biscuits and begins to follow* ALICE's *exercises, stretching out as she stretches.*]

Does you good — bit of exercise.

[*He strains himself on one particular exercise.*]

Oooh — that's a tough one.

[*He sees that* ALICE *is managing it easily enough.*]

Must be easier with a stick.

[*He starts to make conversation which* ALICE *listens to against her will.*]

My daughter Margaret's coming to visit me today. And me grandson, young Damien. What a kid! Nine years old. I tell you, Alice, that boy Damien will grow up to be a great cricketer. He looks just like Greg Chappell — not so tall, though. He's got this bat I bought him. [*Demonstrating*] By Jeez, he can hit that ball.

Young Damien never misses a visit to his old grandpa. You'll see when you meet him, Alice, straightforward, no nonsense with Damien.

MARGARET: [*off*] Dad? Dad?

ALBERT: I'm through here, Margaret.

[MARGARET *enters through the open bathroom door. She carries a bag of things for* ALBERT.]

MARGARET: [*kissing him on the cheek*] Hello, Dad.

ALBERT: Margaret, this is Alice Stoner. She's a doctor.

[*He exits through the bathroom door. There is an awkward pause as* ALICE *and* MARGARET *are left together.*]

ALICE: I'm a botanist. I lecture at the University.

ALBERT: [*off*] And where's that young Damien got to? Damien, where are you, son?

[*He returns.*]

You wait till you meet him, Alice.

MARGARET: Dad . . .

ALBERT: That kid is a natural.

[*He plays a mimed cricket stroke.*]

MARGARET: Dad, Damien couldn't come today. He's playing soccer.

ALBERT: [*stunned*] Soccer? What sort of poofy sport is soccer?

MARGARET: [*embarrassed*] Dad, can't we go and talk outside?

[*She leads him out* ALICE'*s front door, around the set and on to the forestage area.* ALICE *exits into her bathroom.*]

ALBERT: You said he was going to come today.

MARGARET: Dad, he's very busy. He's at school all week and then at weekends he likes to enjoy himself. He's only nine, after all.

ALBERT: I suppose he can't enjoy himself visiting his grandpa?

MARGARET: Of course he loves you, Dad.

ALBERT: You've been turning him against me, haven't you?

MARGARET: No, Dad.

ALBERT: Telling him now that Grandpa's in a home he's gone a bit crazy in the head.

[MARGARET *tries to settle the atmosphere. She takes a packet of biscuits from her bag and gives them to* ALBERT.]

MARGARET: Dad, I've driven for two hours to come and visit you and I didn't come out here to argue.

[ALBERT *pockets the biscuits without even noticing that he has them.*]

ALBERT: I suppose I'm supposed to be grateful.

MARGARET: If you're going to make a scene again I'm going to go.

ALBERT: A two-hour drive. What's a two-hour drive?

MARGARET: I warned you when you moved in, it was too far away.

ALBERT: I'm not a well man.

MARGARET: [*wearily*] I'm going, Dad.

ALBERT: Don't let me hold you up.

MARGARET: [*bursting out*] I don't see why I should keep coming out here week after week just to be abused by you. I'm just sick of your whingeing!

[*Pause.* ALBERT *has been shocked by this.*]

I'm sorry, Dad.

ALBERT: Get out of my sight.

MARGARET: Dad . . .

ALBERT: When I was young children respected their parents.

[MARGARET *sees that he is beyond reason. She takes a child's painting of Greg Chappell from her bag and gives it to him.*]

MARGARET: Damien did this for you at school. He thought

it might be nice for you to hang up in your room. 'Bye,
Dad.

    [*She exits.* ALBERT *waits a moment, then exits and
re-enters* ALICE's *room.* ALICE *enters through the
bathroom door.*]

ALBERT: She called me a whinger. Is that any way to address
your father?

ALICE: Don't you think you might have been a bit hard on
her? It's always easiest to complain to people we're closest
to. But they don't always want to listen.

ALBERT: I've got nothing left to live for.

ALICE: Albert.

ALBERT: Nothing.

ALICE: You don't mean that.

ALBERT: [*looking at his painting*] I wish you could've met
Damien.

ALICE: I will, some day.

    [*She takes his hand.* MATRON *enters and sees what she
imagines to be a little romance blooming.*]

MATRON: Come on, you two. Don't tell me you'd forgotten
the party.

    [*She blows a party whistle.*]

Come on, Albert, down to the dining room. We're just
about to start without you. Come on, Alice.

ALICE: I won't come, thank you, Matron.

MATRON: Oh, but you have to, Alice. It's a party — for the
home's tenth birthday. You have to come. Albert's coming, aren't you, Albert? Of course you are. There's a
chocolate cake, too — your favourite. With cherries.

    [*She plants a party hat on* ALBERT's *head. He exits.*]

Here you are. And here's one for you, Alice.

ALICE: I'm not coming, thank you.

MATRON: Oh, come on, Alice — it will cheer you up.

ALICE: I'm quite happy with my book.

MATRON: Don't be such a spoilsport, Alice. You *have* to
come.

ALICE: I don't *have* to do anything. I'm not coming and
that's that.

MATRON: Have it your own way, then.

    [*She exits.*]

SCENE THREE

Sounds of the party are heard. ALICE *tries to concentrate on her book. A motorbike is heard pulling up.* ALICE *goes to the window and looks out, then hurriedly begins tidying up her room. She exits into the bathroom.* STEVE *and* JULIA *knock at the door, then enter stealthily. Both are dressed outrageously.* STEVE *wears a pith helmet. They realise that* ALICE *is in the bathroom and prepare an elaborate surprise.* ALICE, *now with lipstick on, comes out of the bathroom and is confronted by* JULIA, *pushing a wheelchair around the room while* STEVE *stands on his head on its seat. He bounces out of the wheelchair and raises his safari helmet.*

STEVE: Dr Stoner's living, I presume?

ALICE: [*delighted*] I don't believe it!

JULIA: It took him two weeks to think up that one.

STEVE: It took me two months to find out where she was.

ALICE: I don't believe it. Steve and Julia — my two favourite students! Civilisation at last!

STEVE: I take it you've been missing our intelligent conversation.

ALICE: How on earth did you find me?

JULIA: It wasn't easy. No one at Uni knew where you were. Steve had to go round to your house and wring it out of the neighbours.

STEVE: [*in mock German*] Ve know you are hidink her somevere . . .

ALICE: I didn't mean to have any visitors. Not until I was much better. But it is so good to see you. Thank you so much for coming.

    [*Pause.*]

JULIA: Well, how are you getting on?

ALICE: Oh I'm on the mend, thank you. My hip's still a bit stiff, but I can hobble about. But I am just going crazy in this place. You don't realise how much the simplest things of life mean to you until you can't do them any more. Sometimes I would give anything to be able to cook a curry or vacuum a room or even visit a supermarket. I feel so useless sitting here having everything done for me. Do you remember Norm Fogarty who used to teach in the Department?

JULIA: That was before our time, Dr Stoner.

ALICE: Ah, yes, well, Norm Fogarty was still teaching well into his eighties. Deaf as a post. The students used to do terrible things to him during his lectures but he never noticed. He just went on and on and on, telling the same old stories . . .

[STEVE *and* JULIA *are getting restless.*]

Did I ever tell you about him?

JULIA: No.

STEVE: Yes.

ALICE: I did, didn't I?

JULIA: Yes, you did.

ALICE: Several times too, I expect. I'm sorry — it's just that I miss so much having people to talk to — Good heavens, I'm whingeing! I promised myself that whatever happened I wouldn't whinge. Well, come on, tell me everything. How's Uni? Who's filling in teaching my classes at the moment?

JULIA: We've got this new American lecturer.

STEVE: [*with an American accent*] Dr Daniel Severelli.

ALICE: Severelli? You're privileged — he's one of the Americans' best. How long is he in Australia?

JULIA: I think he's here to stay.

ALICE: Even better. Has he got a job yet?

[STEVE *and* JULIA *are puzzled.*]

STEVE: He's doing your old job.

ALICE: But that's just until I get back. [*Suddenly realising*] Not permanently? He's not doing my job permanently?

JULIA: I think he is.

STEVE: I don't think anyone expected you to come back, Dr Stoner.

ALICE: But I will come back. I must. I can't imagine being stuck in a place like this all my life. It would be just like waiting to die. I'll write to the University — no I'll ring them. I wasn't too old to do the job two months ago. I've only broken my hip.

[*She sinks down into her wheelchair.*]

STEVE: Don't worry about it, Dr Stoner. The important thing for you is just to get well as soon as you can.

[*They rise to leave.*]

ALICE: [*sensing their awkwardness*] I'm really very sorry. It's a bit of a shock, that's all. Thank you for coming to see me.

JULIA: We'll come again.

STEVE: 'Bye.

[*They exit.*]

SCENE FOUR

ALICE *sits, depressed.*

ALBERT: [*offstage, singing*]
    I love my little cat, I do,
    Its coat is oh so warm.
    It comes with me to school each day
    And sits upon the form.
    When teacher says, 'Why do you bring
    That little pet of yours?'
    I tell her that I bring my cat
    Along with me because . . .
    Daddy wouldn't buy me a bow-wow (bow-wow)
    Daddy wouldn't buy me a bow-wow (bow-wow)
    I've got a little cat
    And I'm very fond of that
    But I'd rather have a bow-wow-wow!

[*He enters, wearing his party hat and carrying a piece of chocolate cake on a plate.*]

I saved you a piece of chocolate cake. I got you a bit with a cherry on it.

ALICE: Thank you, Albert.

   [*She takes the cake but doesn't eat it.*]
   Albert, do you like living here?
ALBERT: I don't have any choice. I'm not a well man. I feel
   well, but I'm not.
ALICE: I don't feel old.
ALBERT: Oh, I don't feel old.
ALICE: I feel sick sometimes, or tired. But feeling sick and
   tired feels just the same as it used to feel when I was
   young. Right inside I still feel like the same person I
   always was.
ALBERT: So do I.
ALICE: That's depressing, isn't it? I mean, where's the
   challenge? Where are the new adventures?
   [*Pause*]
ALBERT: If only we had a cat.
ALICE: A what?
ALBERT: A cat. A nice furry little cat.
ALICE: Albert, if your brains were ink there wouldn't be
   enough for a full stop. I'm talking about life, Albert —
   getting out and doing things. You're never too old to start
   something new.
ALBERT: I've never had a cat before.
ALICE: You couldn't have a cat in here. Matron would have
   kittens! [*Laughing*] I can just see you trying to get a cat in
   here, smuggling it in in the dead of night, hiding it under
   the bed ...
ALBERT: Sneaking down the drainpipe to go and buy
   Whiskettes ...
ALICE: Burying Kitty Litter in the garden ...
ALBERT: Operation Cat!
   [*Pause, as they both consider the prospect.*]
ALICE: Albert, I think you should get a cat.
ALBERT: Should I?
ALICE: Yes. If you want one, you should have one.
ALBERT: But you said Matron wouldn't allow it.
ALICE: We needn't tell Matron. It would be a secret cat. No
   one else would know about it.
ALBERT: Just you and me.
ALICE: Just you and me.

[*She takes his hand.*]
ALBERT: Yeah.
[*He exits.*]

SCENE FIVE

MATRON *enters carrying a large box.*

MATRON: I've got a surprise for you, Alice. The man just
brought it.
ALICE: For me?
[*She begins to unpack the box as* MATRON *tidies her
room.*]
MATRON: Oh I've had such a hectic morning. A teacher
came over looking for someone to take care of the school's
guinea pigs at weekends. Well, we asked so many people
but of course no one was really interested.
ALICE: Why ever not?
MATRON: Oh, Alice, you don't know old people the way I
do. Most of the old people here would be quite happy to
sit in their rooms all day if we let them. Feeding guinea
pigs sounds simple enough but it's quite a project for
someone who's getting on a bit. They'd have to find their
way up to the school, go into strange buildings, feed the
guinea pigs just the right amount of just the right things.
And old people do get forgetful, you know. [*Searching*]
There was a card with that somewhere . . . Ah, here it is.
[*She gives it to* ALICE *and then lifts a television set from
the box.*]
Oh, Alice, isn't that lovely! It's from the University.
[*She places the television on a stand in a corner, and
then takes the card out of* ALICE*'s hand and reads it.*]
'To Dr Alice Stoner, in appreciation of forty years'
dedicated work'. Oh, Alice, you must be so proud!
[*She is about to leave when she spots* ALICE*'s chocolate
cake. With a disapproving look she tips the cake into
the box and carries it out. A scratching sound is heard*

from the bathroom. ALICE *takes her stick and moves across to the door. The vent panel falls open.* ALICE *thrusts out her stick and catches* ALBERT, *who has stuck his head through the panel.*]

ALICE: Albert!

ALBERT: Sssh!

ALICE: [*whispering*] What are you doing?

ALBERT: Operation Cat.

[*He stands up and comes through the bathroom door. He then checks to see that no one is listening at the other door.*]

It's a secret escape route for the cat.

ALICE: Really?

ALBERT: Suppose I've got the cat in my room and someone comes in. The cat needs a way to escape into your room without anyone seeing it. I'll show you.

[*He shows* ALICE *a rope made from ties, pyjama cords, etc., which is protruding from the vent on the bathroom door.*

When I knock three times, you call 'Kitty, Kitty, Kitty' and pull the rope.

[*He exits through the bathroom.*]

I'm in my room now. Can you hear me?

ALICE: Yes.

[ALBERT *knocks three times.*]

Kitty, Kitty, Kitty!

[*She pulls the rope through the bathroom door. On the end of it is a mock-up of a cat made with a striped pyjama bottom tied in a knot.* ALBERT *re-enters, very pleased with himself.*]

Albert — you're a genius.

ALBERT: I know. And with a bit of practice the cat will learn to do all that itself.

ALICE: Excellent. Now what about food for this cat?

ALBERT: Ah, I've been reading about that. [*Producing a book*] They should have a mixture of dried and tinned food.

ALICE: But where are you going to store all the food?

ALBERT: I hadn't thought of that.

ALICE: Fortunately, I have. And I've found the perfect hiding place.

[ALBERT *follows her eyes to the television set.*]

Hand me a screwdriver.

[*Together they force the back off the television set and pull out handfuls of wires and bulbs.*]

ALBERT: You've ruined your TV set.

ALICE: All in a good cause.

[*She empties her overnight bag onto the floor and hands it to* ALBERT.]

Now — go and get some tins of cat food. And don't let anyone see you.

ALBERT: Right.

[*He exits.* ALICE *collects the television works and is about to take them to the bathroom.* MATRON *is heard in there, so* ALICE *quickly exits through the other door.* MATRON *enters, singing, then stops. Seeing that there is no one in* ALICE's *room she takes a TV guide and turns on the television. She notices the rope of ties leading into the bathroom.* ALBERT *enters, carrying his bagful of cat food.* MATRON *stuffs TV guide and rope up her blouse. Both want to get out of the room as fast as possible.*]

MATRON: Hello, Albert.

ALBERT: Hello, Matron. Been doing some shopping.

MATRON: Oh, what did you buy?

ALBERT: Just some tins of . . . groceries . . . I'll just put them in my room.

MATRON: Good.

[*They both rush for the doors,* ALBERT *to the bathroom,* MATRON *to the other door. They exit, pause, and both re-enter thinking that the other has gone. Both stop in surprise.*]

ALBERT: Hello, Matron.

MATRON: Hello, Albert.

[*They exit again. This time* ALBERT *returns alone. He transfers the cat food from his bag to the television set and exits through the bathroom. As soon as this door shuts,* MATRON *enters and goes to the television.*

Unable to get a picture, she fiddles with the back and finds the cat food inside.]

'New Whiskas Kidneys and Meat' . . . 'Go-Cat Fish Dinner' . . . 'Snappy Tom Pilchards in Aspic'.

[ALBERT *returns.* MATRON *quickly replaces the tins and the back of the television set.* ALBERT *is carrying a length of rope, which he hides under his cardigan.*]

Hello, Albert. I just brought Alice a TV guide.

ALBERT: Oh. I just brought Alice some rope.

[*He hurriedly stuffs the rope up his cardigan again. They are both very close to the television set.* ALBERT *is terrified that she will discover what is inside.*]

MATRON: Albert, do you get enough to eat here?

ALBERT: Yes — well, I like to store a few things away. In case I get hungry during the night.

MATRON: I see.

ALBERT: Always done it. I think it started during the war.

MATRON: I didn't know you were in the war, Albert?

ALBERT: Too right I was. Don't talk about it much, though. I spent most of my time in a prisoner-of-war camp.

MATRON: [*backing away*] Oh, Albert, I *quite* understand.

[*She exits.* ALBERT *ties the rope to the shopping bag, and then lowers it out the window. The door opens and he quickly drags it all back inside.* ALICE *enters.* ALBERT *shoves his head inside the shopping bag.*]

ALICE: Albert!

ALBERT: Oh, Alice. Operation Cat!

ALICE: But . . .

ALBERT: When I get a cat, we can't just carry it in through the front door. We'll have to put it in the bag and pull it up through the window when it gets dark.

ALICE: Albert, you're a genius!

ALBERT: I know.

ALICE: Come on, let's try it.

[*They lower the bag out of the window, hooking it over the branch of the tree.*]

The rope's too short. It hasn't even reached the first floor.

ALBERT: We'll have to add something on the end . . .

ALICE: My ankle bandage — that's strong and stretchy!

[*She begins to unwind the bandage from her leg as* ALBERT *ties it on to the rope.*]

ALBERT: Good thinking, Ninety-nine!

ALICE: Pardon?

ALBERT: From *Get Smart*.

[*He pulls the ankle bandage, which is still attached to* ALICE's *foot. This brings her wheelchair flying across the room. She crashes into* ALBERT's *back.*]

Sorry, Alice.

ALICE: Sorry, Albert.

ALBERT: We'd better test it for strength. I'll go down and put something in the bag.

ALICE: Right!

ALBERT: I'll give three tugs on the rope when I'm ready.

ALICE: Three tugs on the rope. Right.

[ALBERT *exits.* ALICE *waits and then begins to pay out the rope.*]

ALBERT: [*off*] What's happening up there?

ALICE: The rope's stuck.

ALBERT: [*off*] Give it a flick.

[ALICE *tries to free the rope. There is a knock at her door. Quickly she throws the rope out of the window, but is left clutching the branch of the tree.* MATRON *enters.*]

MATRON: Hello Alice, I was just wondering if . . . That's a nice tree, isn't it?

ALICE: *Grevillea robusta.*

MATRON: [*sensing something offensive*] I beg your pardon?

ALICE: It's a silky oak. *Grevillea robusta's* its proper name.

MATRON: Were you talking to someone? I'm sure I heard voices.

ALICE: Actually, I was talking to the tree. You should talk to plants, you know. Its makes them grow much better. [*Stroking the tree*] You do have nice green leaves today, don't you, Eric. I call this one Eric.

MATRON: Really?

ALICE: [*releasing the tree*] Well, bye-bye, Eric!

MATRON: You do miss your plants, don't you, Alice?

ALICE: Very much, Matron.

MATRON: I think I might be able to do something about that. I think I know just the ticket. Bye-bye, Alice.

[*She turns to go. The tree starts to shake violently.*]

ALBERT: [*off*] Hey, have you forgotten about me out here?

[MATRON *turns to look at the tree, then at* ALICE.]

ALICE: Bye-bye, Matron.

MATRON: [*waving to the tree*] Bye-bye, Eric.

[*She exits hurriedly.* ALICE *goes to the telephone and dials.*]

ALICE: [*into the phone*] Hello, could I speak to Steve or Julia, please? Hello, Steve, it's Alice Stoner speaking. I need you to do me a favour ... tomorrow night ... Well, perhaps you could have your appendix out another night. Now listen, tomorrow afternoon a friend of mine is going to bring you a cat. His name's Albert ... No, my friend's called Albert; the cat hasn't got a name yet. Now this is what you do ...

[*She continues speaking as* ALBERT *enters with the rope tangled about his head.* ALICE *hangs up.*]

ALBERT: What is happening up here?

ALICE: It's all under control. You can get a cat tomorrow.

ALBERT: Tomorrow? Where do I get one?

ALICE: From the stray cats' home. They give away lots of cats that nobody wants. You pick up a cat from there and take it to these people here ... [*Writing on a piece of paper*] They're a couple of my students.

ALBERT: But the cat's supposed to be for us.

ALICE: Steve and Julia are helping us. They'll bring the cat around here and put it in the bag when it gets dark.

ALBERT: Alice, that's very clever.

ALICE: Thank you, Albert.

ALBERT: I think this is going to work.

ALICE: So do I.

[ALBERT *hesitates for a moment, and then gives her a kiss. She is at first taken aback, then pleased.* ALBERT *exits. Music.* ALICE *draws the curtains shut.*]

SCENE SIX

MATRON *enters. Behind her back she holds a very spiky cactus in a small pot.*

MATRON: Good morning, Alice.
ALICE: Good morning, Matron.
MATRON: [*waving to the tree*] Good morning, Eric.
ALICE: Come on, Eric — say good morning to the nice lady. He's very shy today, Matron.
MATRON: [*presenting the cactus*] I've brought you a little present, Alice.
ALICE: Oh, Matron, how kind of you! Isn't he lovely? What's his name?
MATRON: Oh . . . er, Nigel.
ALICE: Nigel — what a lovely name! Isn't it, Nigel? Hello, Nigel.
MATRON: [*coming to the point*] Have you seen Albert to-day, Alice?
ALICE: I think he went out somewhere.
MATRON: You don't know where?
ALICE: He didn't say.
MATRON: He didn't take any . . . food with him?
ALICE: I don't know, Matron.
    [MATRON *is trying to look at the television.*]
MATRON: You're lucky to have such a nice TV set.
ALICE: Oh, I hardly ever watch it.
MATRON: [*moving towards the television*] Isn't it working properly? Perhaps I could . . .
ALICE: Matron!
MATRON: Yes?
ALICE: Er . . . Nigel wants a kiss.
MATRON: Pardon?
ALICE: Isn't that sweet, Matron? Nigel wants you to give him a kiss.
MATRON: [*trying to laugh it off*] But Nigel's so spiky, Alice.

ALICE: He'll be very offended if you don't. Won't you, Nigel?

    [MATRON *purses her lips and for a moment it looks as if Nigel will get his kiss, but it is too much for her.*]

MATRON: I'm very busy today, Nigel. Bye-bye. [*Waving*] Bye-bye, Eric.

    [*She exits. Music.*]

SCENE SEVEN

ALICE *prepares a small celebration in her room, putting out a bottle of wine and two cups. She glances at her watch, then out of the window. There is a knock at the door and* ALBERT *enters.*

ALICE: Where have you been? You missed dinner and everything!

ALBERT: [*evasively*] It . . . took longer than I thought.

ALICE: Did you find a cat at the cats' home?

ALBERT: Yes, a really nice one. Ginger.

ALICE: And you didn't get lost on the way to Steve and Julia's?

ALBERT: No, no trouble there.

ALICE: Well done, Albert. See — it's not so hard to do things after all, is it? What time did they say they'd bring the cat?

ALBERT: We . . . didn't make any definite arrangement.

ALICE: It doesn't matter, Albert, I'm sure they'll use their common sense. We'll just have to keep a lookout for them. [*Opening the bottle of wine*] Right — let's celebrate our success!

ALBERT: I'm not supposed to drink. I'm not a well man.

ALICE: Oh, come on, Albert, it's a special occasion. Anyway, after all you've been through you've earned it.

    [*She pours them each a drink in the cups.*]

    To Operation Cat!

ALBERT: To Operation Cat.

[*They drink.*]

ALICE: Now, tell me everything. What happened?

ALBERT: There's not much to tell.

ALICE: Albert, this is my adventure too, you know. I want to know all about it.

ALBERT: Alice, there's something I should tell you . . .

[*A motorbike is heard approaching.*]

ALICE: Sssh! Listen!

ALBERT: What is it?

ALICE: A motorbike. That will be Steve and Julia with the cat.

[*She looks out of the window. The motorbike stops.*]

Yes, it is them — help me get the rope out the window.

[*She begins to lower the rope. There is a knock at the door.*]

MATRON: [*off*] Alice? Alice, have you seen Albert?

[ALICE *opens the door and* MATRON *enters.*]

He wasn't at dinner and he's not in his room . . . Oh, there you are, Albert! Oh, I'm so relieved. You mustn't ever run away again!

[ALBERT *makes a dash for the bathroom door and exits through it.*]

Alice — stop him!

ALICE: What's happening, Matron?

MATRON: Oh, Alice, Albert's terribly confused. He thinks he's in a prisoner of war camp. He's trying to escape.

[*She exits through the bathroom door. As soon as she is gone,* ALBERT *enters through the front door.*]

ALBERT: I think I've lost her. Now come on, help me get the bag up.

[*Together they pull up the rope. As* MATRON *bursts in through the front door, they throw the bag out of the window.*]

MATRON: Now, Albert, just stay where you are. It's quite all right . . .

[ALBERT *dashes through the bathroom door again.* MATRON *chases him but he slams the door in her face, dealing her a fearsome blow on the nose. She recovers her composure, then runs through the door.* ALICE *begins to haul up the bag, but stops as* MATRON *returns through her front door.*]

Alice, remain abso-lutely calm! Poor Albert — he's been planning all this for some time. He tunnelled through your bathroom door and filled your TV set with cat food.

ALICE: Cat food?

MATRON: Oh, I think it must remind him of the food he had in prison camp. He was planning to put the food in a bag and make his escape by climbing through your window . . .

[*She notices the rope, which is beginning to snake back out of the window, as* ALBERT *pulls it from below.*]

Through the window! Alice, I have to stop him!

ALBERT: [*off*] Is Matron still up there?

MATRON: [*shocked*] I haven't got time for you, Eric! Or you, Nigel!

[*She exits.* ALICE *pulls up the bag.*]

ALICE: Kitty, Kitty, Kitty . . .

[MATRON *re-enters through the bathroom door, while* ALICE *desperately conceals the bag.* MATRON, *carrying* ALBERT'*s dressing gown, motions to* ALICE *to keep quiet, then conceals herself by the bathroom door.* ALBERT *enters through this door.*]

ALBERT: Alice, there's something I have to tell you . . .

[MATRON *throws the dressing gown over* ALBERT'*s head and holds it in position.*]

MATRON: Got you! Now, Albert, there's no need to worry, it's Matron here. You just stay here and I'll bring you a nice tablet. Hold him, Alice!

[*She passes the trussed* ALBERT *into* ALICE'*s arms and rushes out.* ALICE *frees* ALBERT.]

ALBERT: She's mad!

ALICE: Heavens — the cat!

[*She fumbles with the bag and opens it. Pause.*]

You didn't get a cat, did you, Albert?

[ALBERT *shakes his head.*]

You said you did. You said . . . what went wrong?

ALBERT: I went to the stray cats' home. They were very nice to me. We went and picked out a lovely little cat, a ginger

one. And then they asked me 'Where do you live?' and I
said 'Renby Road Retirement Hostel' and they said 'Have
— you — got — permission?'
[*Pause.*]
ALICE: Well, that's that, then. You could have told me,
Albert.
ALBERT: Do you know what happens to stray cats? If
nobody wants them they put them to sleep. They think it's
kinder to put them to sleep than to send them to live here.
[*Pause.*]
I must have been mad to think we could do it. What sort
of life would it be for a cat all cooped up here in one
room. It wouldn't be fair to anyone.
ALICE: I know.
[*She takes his hand.* MATRON *enters with a pill and a
glass of water.*]
MATRON: Now, Albert — just take this tablet . . .
ALICE: Calm down, Matron — Albert's quite all right.
MATRON: Don't be silly, Alice. You can see what he was
doing.
ALICE: No, Matron. He had quite a clever plan, really.
ALBERT: We wanted to get a cat.
MATRON: A cat? In here?
ALICE: It was a secret operation. We were going to hide the
cat in here and feed it with the food we kept in the televi-
sion. We were going to bring it in through the window
tonight.
MATRON: Oh, I see. You've been fooling me. Oh, you two
have made such a fool of me. That really was very clever.
[*She swallows the tablet herself and washes it down with
the water.*]
I'm sorry. You really can't have a cat in here.
ALBERT: We know.
MATRON: [*for the first time talking to them as if they were
adults*] There are so many people living in the hostel.
Some of the them like cats, some of them don't. And what
if everyone wanted to keep a pet? We have to have some
rules, otherwise . . .
ALICE: Matron, we quite understand.

ALBERT: It just gave us something exciting to do.

ALICE: I'm sorry if it caused you so much trouble. But sometimes we just get so . . . bored and useless.

MATRON: I know. Sometimes *I* feel that I'm . . . I get so busy keeping everyone fed, keeping the place clean and tidy, that I forget there are more important things. I just wish that I could find something else for you.

[*Pause.*]

What about those guinea pigs?

ALBERT: Guinea pigs?

MATRON: You remember, Alice — the school was looking for someone to take care of their guinea pigs at weekends.

ALICE: Oh, yes.

[*She and* ALBERT *look doubtfully at each other.*]

MATRON: Oh, I know it doesn't sound very exciting but it would be a big help to them.

ALBERT: There's a chapter in my pet book about guinea pigs.

[*He leafs through his book, then stops.*]

And snakes. Do you think the school would like to keep a snake?

MATRON: I don't know, Albert.

ALBERT: Not a poisonous one — a carpet snake or a green tree snake. They're very interesting. The kids could learn about hibernation.

ALICE: If we took the front off the television and put in some clear glass it would make a wonderful snake box.

MATRON: I'd better ring the school about it.

ALICE: Oh would you, Matron, Thank you.

[MATRON *exits.* ALICE *and* ALBERT *take the cat food from the television.*]

ALBERT: Snakes need frogs to eat. And mice.

ALICE: And guinea pigs.

ALBERT: Alice!

ALICE: I think I could get some from the University.

ALBERT: They don't eat much. One mouse will keep a snake going for quite a long time.

ALICE: Albert?

ALBERT: Yes?

ALICE: It's fun, isn't it, having adventures?
ALBERT: Yes.
ALICE: I like adventures.
ALBERT: So do I.
[*Music.* ALICE *steps forward as* ALBERT *continues working at the television set.*]
ALICE: [*to the audience*] Sooner or later, we all grow old. Sometimes old people need special help, even special places to live. But the important things we need are the same things we always needed: challenges, adventures, new things to learn. We need to feel wanted and useful. And we need friends . . .
[*She takes* ALBERT's *hand.*]
. . . and special friends.
[MATRON *enters.*]
MATRON: Come on, you two.
[*She leads them both forward. All bow.*]

THE END

Wolf Boy

Peter Charlton

Above: Peter Gray and Jai McHenry; below: Rick Ireland, Russell Thomson, Jai McHenry and James Cox in the Arena Theatre Company production of *Wolf Boy*. Photos by Peter Charlton.

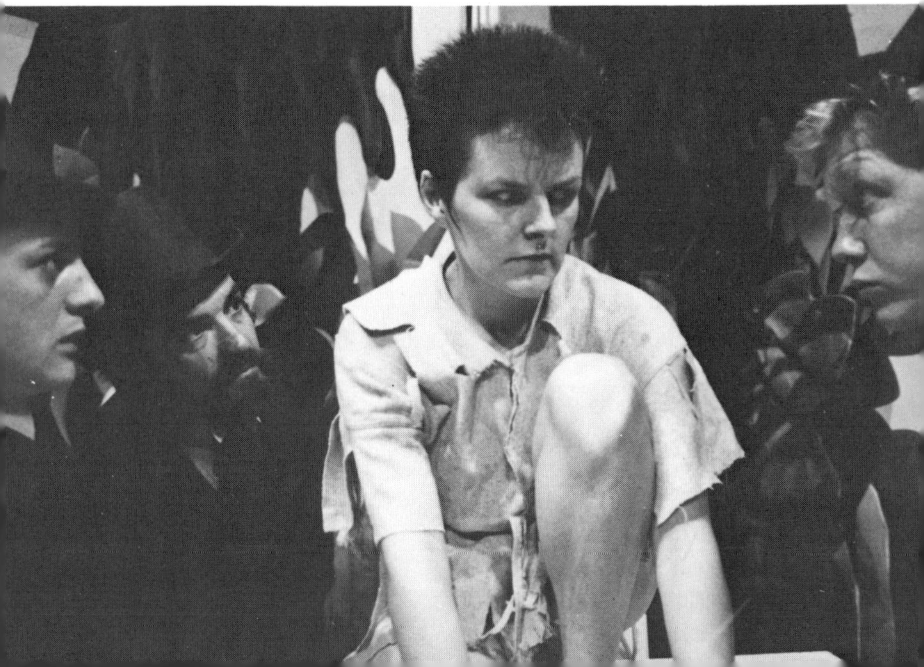

FOREWORD

Wolf Boy is a very free interpretation of the only well-documented case of the capture and study of a feral, or wild, child.

In 1800, in a forest near Aveyron in France, 'Victor' (as he was later called) was captured. All early attempts to communicate with him were fruitless, his responses to stimuli being unpredictable and erratic. He quickly became a victim of the chaotic bureaucracy in post-revolutionary France, and was incarcerated in the Paris Institute for Deaf-Mutes while decisions were being made about his future.

It was here that Jean-Marc-Gaspard Itard, defying the attitudes of his superiors, undertook the education of Victor. His approach to the task was a breakthrough in both the methodology and philosophy of education, being the first-ever attempt to structure a learning process to suit the particular needs of an individual student in a learning institution. Itard worked with Victor for five years, and as well as providing two long and comprehensive reports on his progress, kept a diary which contained details of his methodology, which has had enormous repercussions in all Western education systems. Maria Montessori was profoundly influenced by Itard and all modern education is deeply indebted to him.

I chose this story for two reasons — first, I had long wanted to work on a TIE project about the process of education, as opposed to individual or personal dilemmas within that process; and, second, I felt that the story of Victor was an ideal vehicle with which I could attempt a 'new' approach to TIE work.

After working in TIE and related areas for many years, I had begun to feel that a uniformity of both style and form had evolved which no longer suited my own political expression. I wanted to break with the practice of presenting a single issue in either a naturalistic or muted agit-prop style. What I sought instead was to place the issue of the play in a much broader context and examine a wide range of social and political questions. In this I was guided by the writings of the Italian Marxist theorist Antonio Gramsci, whose understanding of the political and cultural functions of state institutions is, I feel, of particular relevance to TIE.

The story of Victor contained many elements which were perfect for an expression of some of Gramsci's ideas — there is the question of the role of the intellectual in society, the relationships between 'rulers' and 'ruled', the function of institutions, especially the bureaucracy, the family and the education system, the rights of the individual to dignity and self-esteem, and so on. But most importantly, it clearly allowed for a strong visual or theatrical interpretation of these things, while also demanding a non-naturalistic style in order to present difficult and complex ideas to young children.

All of these things (and more) I endeavoured to mould carefully into an 'objective' analysis of Victor and his situation. What I failed to anticipate was the power of the story really to move people, especially adults. Many feel that Victor's life was tragic, but if that is so, then so must all our lives be, for what was done to him, is still done to us all. For all his advances in technique, Itard was still a 'traditional' intellectual, enslaved by the moral and cultural values of his ruling class, lamely challenging them, but still seeking their approbation. Through him, Victor was being patterned according to certain held beliefs which were 'unchallengeable', and that is the true tragedy, not only for Victor, but for all children in all schools.

Peter Charlton, May, 1984

PETER CHARLTON was born in Perth, Western Australia, in 1947. He trained as a teacher and taught briefly in primary and secondary schools in Western Australia, Victoria and South Australia.

While a student he began performing as a singer and appeared regularly on Perth television. In 1967 he worked for the first time with children and since then has worked extensively in TIE and Youth Theatre as a performer, writer, musician, director, designer and teacher.

In 1981 he was appointed Artistic Director of Arena Theatre in Melbourne, and began to investigate new ways of approaching theatre in education. *Wolf Boy* is the third play to emerge from that continuing investigation.

Wolf Boy was first performed by the Arena Theatre Company at the Arena Theatre, Melbourne on 14 June 1982 with the following cast:

VICTOR (WOLF BOY)	Wendy Gale
TEACHER	Mark Morrissey
PARENT	Lynne Ruthven
CHORUS 1	John Bayliss
CHORUS 2	Paul Chapple
CHORUS 3	Kath Herbert

Directed by Peter Charlton
Designed by Kenneth Evans

CHARACTERS

VICTOR, THE WOLF BOY
TEACHER
PARENT
THREE GENTLEMEN OF THE CHORUS

SETTING

A jungle capable of transforming into a room.

WOLF BOY

On a table in the centre of the performing area, the WOLF
BOY *sits, covered completely by a black cape. Occasionally
he moves so that the audience is aware of his presence.
Three chairs are around the table, but in no order. At the
front of the playing area is a box containing all the props
needed for the play. Wherever possible the props and furniture are white and clinical.*

When the audience has settled, the actors of the CHORUS
*enter. They are all dressed in top hats and tails. They move
with elegant economy and arrange the three chairs across
the space. They sit correctly and mime opening books.
Their speeches are accompanied by — and punctuated with
— clear gestures which relate directly to what they say. This
gesture language is used during all their chorus work, but
stops, or is used minimally for emphasis, during the se-
quences involving characterisation.*

CHORUS 1: Once upon a time/In the deep, dark forest
CHORUS 2: Far, far away/Where people dare not go
CHORUS 3: There lived/There lived
CHORUS 1: *A creature!*
> [*They stop gesturing and all stand, agitated and afraid.
> They are local villagers.*]
CHORUS 2: What sort of creature?
CHORUS 3: Where?
CHORUS 2: What do you mean?
CHORUS 3: What sort of creature?
CHORUS 1: It looks like . . .
CHORUS 2: Yes?
CHORUS 3: Yes?
CHORUS 1: A human child!
CHORUS 2: In the forest?
CHORUS 3: Impossible.
CHORUS 2: How did it get there?

CHORUS 3: You're dreaming.

CHORUS 2: Seeing things.

CHORUS 2 and 3: A child could not live in the forest.

CHORUS 1: I said it *looks* like a child, but it runs ... like ... a wolf!

CHORUS 2: *No.*

CHORUS 3: You're going crazy. Hunters' madness.

CHORUS 2: All hunters see things. It's just a day-dream.

CHORUS 3: Alone in the forest, your mind plays tricks. Makes you see things that aren't really there.

CHORUS 1: I tell you it *is* there. And if you come with me you will see for yourselves that it is. I have seen it many times and know where it lives. Perhaps we could even capture it.

> [*They remove their hats and coats, leaving them neatly on their chairs. They group together and move cautiously towards the central table, gesturing silence and caution.*
>
> CHORUS 1 *signals* CHORUS 2 *and* 3 *to move out to surround the table. They sneak about, half-crouched, half-terrified. They wait a moment.*]

Now!!

> [*All three pounce on the shape beneath the black cape. There is a dreadful howl.* CHORUS 2 *and* 3 *run from the shape, holding ropes. The shape struggles violently.* CHORUS 1 *spins round to the audience while* CHORUS 2 *and* 3 *struggle with the ropes.*]

Roll up, roll up. Ladies and gentlemen, roll up and see a sight that will amaze and astound you. A creature you have only dreamed about until now. Captured this very day by three brave hunters of this village who risked their lives to bring here this — *thing.* A human. And yet not human. An animal. And yet not animal. A human child. A boy — a *Wolf Boy.*

> [*He pulls the cloth from* WOLF BOY. *The struggling has stopped and the* WOLF BOY *crouches, staring blankly ahead. Still, silent and terrified. Slowly he opens his mouth into a silent call for help, one hand reaching forward.*]

[*striking at the* WOLF BOY] Back! Back!

CHORUS 2: What are we going to do with him?

CHORUS 3: We can't keep him here.

CHORUS 2: Just another mouth to feed.

CHORUS 3: Maybe we should let him go.

CHORUS 2: To run free in the forest.

CHROUS 3: That's the life he's used to.

CHORUS 1: But we have saved him from that. We must now do the correct thing.

CHORUS 2 and 3: What's that?

CHORUS 1: We must tell the authorities.

CHORUS: [*gesturing*] When there's a problem,
    When there's a doubt,
    Go straight to the authorities,
    They'll sort things out.
    The authorities know everything.
    At least, they think they do.
    And they're very useful people
    When you don't know what to do.

[CHORUS 1 *repeats the whole movement sequence while* CHORUS 2 *and* 3 *put on their coats and hats. They assume the pompous air of local government officials.*]

CHORUS 2: And you found him in the forest?

CHORUS 1: Yes, sir.

CHORUS 3: And you captured him yourself?

CHORUS 1: Yes, sir.

CHORUS 2: And you want us to decide what to do?

CHORUS 1: Yes, sir.

CHORUS 3: Bring it here.

CHORUS 1: But, sir!

CHORUS 2: We need to see it if we are to decide what to do.

CHORUS 1: But, sir. . .

CHORUS 3: Bring it *here*.

[CHORUS 1 *goes to the table; gathers up the ropes and holds them as a leash. He tugs gently and calls to the* WOLF BOY. *There is no response.*]

CHORUS 1: He won't come.

CHORUS 2: He's terrified, poor thing.

CHORUS 3: Untie him. He can't get out of the room.

[CHORUS 1 *carefully unties the ropes and steps back, the* WOLF BOY *is silent, motionless. The others all lean forward for a closer look. Suddenly, the* WOLF BOY *leaps into action, trying to escape from the room. The* CHORUS, *terrified, group together for protection. The* WOLF BOY *moves gracefully, his body in perfect control. The* CHORUS *are clumsy and do not work as a team. It is like a slapstick silent movie chase. The chase ends as suddenly as it started, with the* WOLF BOY *crouching, staring straight ahead, growling.*]

CHORUS 1: You see, sirs. He is wild, untamed and listen to the sounds he makes. Like an animal. Like a wolf.

[*The* WOLF BOY *moans softly and rocks back and forth.* CHORUS 2 *and* 3 *move aside in urgent discussion.*]

CHORUS 2: I don't like it. It's dangerous for us to decide. Yesterday there was no problem. This thing, this child, ran free in the forest and caused no trouble. It seems to me that the whole problem could be solved by putting the boy back where he came from.

CHORUS 3: But wait. We must be careful. The fact is that the boy has been caught and brought to us. What a rare thing he is. How many scientists, doctors, teachers and many others would be interested in him? He is too important for us to decide. We must do the correct thing.

CHORUS 2 and 3: Send him to a more important authority!
[*gesturing*] When there's a problem,
>> When there's a doubt,
>> Go straight to the authorities,
>> They'll sort things out.
>> The authorities know everything.
>> At least, they think they do.
>> And they're very useful people.
>> When you don't know what to do.

[CHORUS 2 *and* 3 *repeat the movement sequence.* CHORUS 1 *puts on his hat and coat and assumes an absurdly pompous bearing.*]

CHORUS 2: And so we brought him to you, sir —

CHORUS 3: without delay —

CHORUS 2: hoping that you —

CHORUS 3: being so important —
CHORUS 2 and 3: might know what to do.
CHORUS 1: I see. And have you examined the boy
   carefully?
CHORUS 2: Um, no, sir. We, er —
CHORUS 3: We thought it best to wait for you to see him,
   sir.
CHORUS 1: I see. Well, gentlemen, bring him here and
   we shall examine him.
   [*The* WOLF BOY *is pulled back onto the table and all
   three crowd around to examine him.*]
Definitely a human boy-child.
CHORUS 2: No clothes. Disgraceful!
CHORUS 3: Covered in scars.
CHORUS 1: Ten or eleven years old.
CHORUS 2: Runs on all fours.
CHORUS 3: Makes animal sounds. Can't speak.
CHORUS 1: *Or* can't hear. Maybe we need to test further.
   [*Speaking slowly and carefully*] What . . . is . . . your . . .
   name?
   [*No response.*]
CHORUS 2: Where . . . do . . . you . . . come from?
CHORUS 3: Who are your parents?
CHORUS 1: How many fingers?
CHORUS 2: What colour is my tie?
CHORUS 3: Where is the window?
   [*Their questions become louder and more frantic.*]
CHORUS 1: Two plus two?
CHORUS 2: Spell 'cat'.
CHORUS 3: What is the capital of France?
CHORUS 1: How many days in a week?
CHORUS 2: What time is it?
CHORUS 3: What is the . . .?
CHORUS 1: Where are the . . .?
CHORUS 2: How can we . . .?
CHORUS 3: Where?
CHORUS 1: When?
CHORUS 2: Who?
CHORUS 3: How?

CHORUS 1, 2 and 3: Why?

> [*As soon as they stop, the* WOLF BOY *begins to laugh.
> Softly at first, then growing into beautiful, innocent
> laughter. His face remains blank, showing no emotion
> or expression. The* CHORUS *look on aghast. The* WOLF
> BOY *stops and sits silently, staring straight ahead.*]

CHORUS 1: It is obvious, gentlemen, that the child is
an idiot. Doesn't understand a thing. Deaf. Dumb. And
stupid.

CHORUS 2: It is obvious, gentlemen, that the child
was left in the forest by his parents because he was an
idiot. They left him to die, but somehow he survived and
lived with animals — wolves.

CHORUS 3: It is obvious, gentlemen, that an idiot could
not survive alone in the forest. We have just had the
coldest winter since ninety-five. The child must have *some*
sense in order to live for probably years in the forest. He
just *seems* like an idiot because he's forgotten how to
behave like a human.

CHORUS 1: Maybe you're right. I don't know.

CHORUS 2: I think he's an idiot. It's plain for all to see.

CHORUS 3: Well, if we can't agree, then we must do the
correct thing.

CHORUS 1: Yes, yes. The correct thing.

CHORUS 2: It must be done.

CHORUS 3: We must take him to an expert ...

CHORUS 1, 2 and 3: A genius, a specialist, a star.
Someone who knows more than us by far!
But who do we turn to, where do we go
To find the right person, who's certain to know?
A doctor?
A lawyer?
A scientist?
A priest?
Just how many people are experts on beasts?

> [CHORUS 1 *and* 2 *repeat the gestures for doctor, lawyer,
> scientist and priest, saying the word with each sign. The
> sequence is repeated several times, during which*
> CHORUS 3 *mounts the table. The* CHORUS *stops on the*

word 'doctor' and CHORUS 3 *speaks as an extremely
learned doctor, old and respected in his profession.*]

CHORUS 3: For six weeks now this Wolf Boy has been in my
care. I have studied him closely so that his future can be
decided. Can he become a normal human being? Is he
really wild? Is he an idiot? I was asked to answer all these
questions.

[*During the next part of the speech the* WOLF BOY
*moves off the table and moves in a sort of dance to the
words, sometimes agreeing with what is said, sometimes
questioning, sometimes joking.*]

And what have I seen? He can walk on two feet, but not
like us. He runs on all fours and is graceful to watch. His
senses are strange.

[CHORUS 1 *and* 2 *assist the* WOLF BOY's *dance with
appropriate gestures, actions or props.*]

He is not blind — he can run quickly without bumping
into things. But he does not seem to see things held in
front of his eyes. He stares blankly ahead. He is not deaf.
But when a gun is fired near him, he does not hear it. Yet,
fill a glass with water and no matter how quietly you do it,
he turns to look for the water to drink. He doesn't know
hot from cold. I have seen him put his hand into boiling
water to get a potato to eat, and not feel a thing. Like a
cat or a dog he can sleep close to a large fire and then
walk outside into the cold night air. He doesn't speak.

[*The* WOLF BOY's *dance is interrupted by the last statement. The* WOLF BOY *and* CHORUS 2 *and* 3 *stop.*]

He is an idiot.

[*The* WOLF BOY *falls to the floor*]

A hopeless case. Incurable. He will never be civilised.

[CHORUS 1 *and* 2 *take* WOLF BOY *back to the table,
repeating the word 'civilised'. All three* CHORUS
*perform the following with immaculate finesse and
precision.*]

CHORUS: If it's civilised you want to be
      You can do no better than be like me
      Polite, well-spoken, so refined;
      A healthy body, a healthy mind.

And I know what's right and wrong
I can even sing a song
And it cannot be disguised
That I'm very civilised
    Yes, I'm civilised,
    Yes, I'm civilised.
And I always eat with a knife and fork.
I know when to listen and when to talk.
Polite, well-mannered, so refined;
A healthy body, a healthy mind.
And I know what's good and bad
And I know what's sane and mad
And by now you've realised
That I'm very civilised.

[*They repeat the above in a formalised gesture dance. During this the* TEACHER *and the* PARENT *enter. They are in deep discussion, which slowly increases in volume until, at the end of the dance the conversation can be clearly heard.*]

PARENT: ... but if everyone thinks he is a hopeless case, then why do you want to bother with him? It's a waste of time and effort.

TEACHER: But I think they are all wrong. If I had the chance to teach him — and no one has tried yet — I think I could change him from a savage into a normal human child. If we worked together we could achieve a miracle. We could prove that they are all wrong.

PARENT: But what if what they say is true? What if he really is a fake, an idiot? Besides I'm too busy to waste my time ... I'm your house-keeper, not your assistant ...

TEACHER: Just imagine, though, how famous we could both be. The whole world would know. Doctors, scientists, all sorts of people would visit us — and the Wolf Boy.

PARENT: Well, I don't know. It seems like a lot of trouble — and you don't even know if your teaching will work.

TEACHER: At least let us try. Please. Come with me to see the boy and then decide. Come on. It can't do any harm.

    [*They turn to face the* WOLF BOY, *who is asleep on the*

table. All three CHORUS *stand between them. They are
now brutish gaolers.*]

CHORUS 1: Can't you get it into your head. The boy is a
hopeless case. An idiot.

CHORUS 2: You won't do yourselves any good by sticking
your noses into matters that don't concern you.

CHORUS 1: Keep away.

CHORUS 2: Stay out.

CHORUS 1: It's none of your business.

TEACHER: But all I — we — want to do is have a look at
him. Closely.

CHORUS 2: He's dangerous.

CHORUS 1: He bites.

CHORUS 2: He's filthy.

CHORUS 1: No clothes.

CHORUS 2: Sleeps in his own mess.

CHORUS 1: Stinks.

CHORUS 2: Ugly.

CHORUS 1: Dangerous.

CHORUS 1 and 2: A stinking, ugly, dangerous idiot.

CHORUS 1: No one can help him.

PARENT: And has anyone tried to help him? Has anyone given him love and care?

TEACHER: He's locked away in a dark room. A prisoner.
All I am asking for is the chance to set him free. To care
for him and to teach him. Everyone calls him an idiot —
but no one has even tried to teach him the things we have
all learned.

PARENT: You call yourselves civilised. And yet you treat
a child so cruelly. Who is savage?: an innocent boy, or
grown men who should know better?

CHORUS 3: Maybe they're right. It will do him no harm
to have people care for him. And some good might come
of it. Anyway it would be a relief to be rid of him.

[*The three* CHORUS *stand aside and the* TEACHER *and
the* PARENT *move slowly towards the table. They mime
opening a door and looking inside.*]

TEACHER: It's so dark, I can't see a thing.

PARENT: There he is — in the corner over there.

TEACHER: The smell! I think I'm going to be sick.
PARENT: Wait here, then, and I'll get him.
> [*She moves gently towards the* WOLF BOY, *making sounds of reassurance, as though to a cat or dog. She gathers up the ropes and leads him out of the cell.*]
TEACHER: Oh, look at the poor thing. How cruel to let him become like this. So thin, so sickly. So dirty.
PARENT: He can't stay here, no matter what. He'll die soon, for sure. We must take care of him.
TEACHER: Yes, we must.
Together we shall care for him. And together we will prove that the experts are wrong. We will have a great victory.
PARENT: Victory! Yes. And so, we shall call the boy *Victor*.
TEACHER: *Victor*.
CHORUS 1: *Victor*.
CHORUS 2: *Victor*.
CHORUS 3: *Victor*.
> [*With each repetition the boy becomes more aware of his name, laughing and running to whoever has just said it. Then he runs around laughing and leaping.*]
TEACHER: Victor. Come here.
> [*He returns and sits between his two benefactors.*]
CHORUS: We are certainly happy to see him go
And if they can teach him, we'd like to know.
But if they can't — well — we told you so!
> [*They move the table and chairs to a central position to make a conventional set-up. The* TEACHER *sits on the right, the* PARENT *on the left and* VICTOR *in the middle.* VICTOR, *sullen and melancholy, pays no attention to what is said.*]
PARENT: Well. Now we've got him, what do we do?
TEACHER: We care for him as if he were our own child. And we teach him the things he has never learned. Things we don't even think about, because we don't remember how we learnt them.
PARENT: I'm afraid that I will not be able to do it. I've never been to school, I don't know what to do. I haven't

learnt these things you speak of.

TEACHER: Of course you have. You can walk, run, laugh, cry, see, hear, *speak*. Play games, draw pictures, chop wood, cook food — all sorts of things. Now, what do you think should be the first thing we do for our young friend, Victor?

[VICTOR *responds with a look.*]

A bath? Some clean clothes? What?

PARENT: He's so thin. Looks so sick. I think before anything else, a good feed! Victor!

[*He turns to look at her.*]

Are you hungry? Do you want some food?

[*There is no response. She repeats it, with gestures.*]

Are you hungry? Do you want some food?

[VICTOR *looks at her. She repeats the gestures. Hesitantly he signs 'me', 'hungry', 'food', and holds the last gesture, tentative and afraid. The* CHORUS *mimes setting out a sumptuous feast.*]

CHORUS 1: A delicious vegetable soup.

CHORUS 2: Pure, white bread and butter.

CHORUS 3: Roast beef —

CHORUS 1: And vegetables.

CHORUS 2: Strawberries and cream —

CHORUS 3: And coffee.

[*They stand back and wait, eager and expectant. The* TEACHER *and the* PARENT *mime eating, enjoying each mouthful.* VICTOR *sniffs his meal carefully, paying no attention to the other two. He re-commences miming hunger, this time with whines, grunts and howls. He leaves the table and moves energetically around the room. The* CHORUS *is horror-struck.*]

CHORUS 1: Look at that. Shocking.

CHORUS 2: No manners.

CHORUS 3: He's hungry, but won't eat.

TEACHER: Gentlemen. Stop and think.

[*The* PARENT *goes over to* VICTOR *and soothes him.*]

If you lived in the forest, what would you eat?

CHORUS 1: Live in the forest!

CHORUS 2: What an idea!

CHORUS 3: It just couldn't happen.
TEACHER: But, if it happend —
CHORUS 1: It never would.
TEACHER: Just imagine it did.
CHORUS 2: Then the first thing to think of —
CHORUS 3: Would have to be food.
CHORUS: There'd be nuts
            And berries
            And leaves
            And fruits
            And bird's eggs.
            Vegetables
            Mushrooms
            And roots
            And —
TEACHER: But this boy, they say, was living with wolves. What would he have eaten living as a wolf? Try to imagine yourselves as *wolves*.
CHORUS: Wolves
            Fur
            Paws
            Fangs
            Run
            Hunt
            Kill
            Eat
            Blood
            Bones
            Raw
            Meat

[*By the end of the sequence they have become animalistic, carried away by the words and gestures.* CHORUS 1 *regains composure and with a clap snaps the others out of their state. They all pull themselves together and re-set the table.*]

CHORUS 1: Some walnuts, picked this morning.
CHORUS 2: Raw potatoes, straight from the garden.
CHORUS 3: Meat. Uncooked. Raw. Meat.
PARENT: Come on, Victor. Food. Come on.

[VICTOR *races to the table and gobbles the walnuts and
potato. We sniffs each thing before eating it. He eats
some of the meat, but is indifferent to it.*]
Well, we know now what he likes. That's a start.
TEACHER: And now, we can really begin.
CHORUS: [*On the move, gesturing*] In a room, with a
window and door
And a ceiling and walls and a floor,
A new life begins.
In a garden with high walls of stone,
And a pond and a lawn, neatly mown,
A new life begins.
Good luck dear teacher and friend.
We'll return before the end
To see how this new life has grown.
TEACHER: And now to get you cleaned up, young man.
PARENT: A bath, some soap and a good scrub.
[*They set up the bath. It is hot. The* TEACHER *and the*
PARENT *try to get* VICTOR *to the bath. He resists and
when eventually in the bath, struggles violently at first,
perhaps escaping or pulling the* TEACHER *into the
water. He calms down slowly.*]
Now, first we wash the hair.
Then the face, neck, shoulders, arms, chests, tummy,
back, bottom, legs, feet. There!
[VICTOR *comes out of the bath and stands still, then
slowly, carefully feels himself — each part in the order
of washing.*]
TEACHER: And now some clothes.
[*The three* CHORUS *enter carrying clothes and shoes.*]
CHORUS 1: Clothes
CHORUS 2: Make
CHORUS 3: The man.
[*They all crowd around, concealing* VICTOR *from the
audience. There is a continual struggle until the end of
the sequence. Clothes fly about and the names of items
of clothing are called out.*]
Underpants.
Singlet.

Shirt.
Trousers.
Socks.
Tie.
Vest.
Jacket.
Shoes.
Cap.

> [*They step back and look at* VICTOR, *who is dressed like a school boy. Untidy. Uncomfortable. They all admire him.*]

CHORUS 1: Isn't he lovely!

CHORUS 2: Quite the little man.

CHORUS 3: Doesn't he look smart?

CHORUS 1: All dressed up.

CHORUS 2: That's better.

CHORUS 3: What a gentleman.

> [*They are patronising, as though talking to a baby. On each line they move in to him and adjust his clothes until he is neat. They step back once again to admire him.* VICTOR *suddenly and desperately tries to tear the clothes off. He manages to get rid of the jacket, the tie, the shoes and socks and the cap, throwing them at the others. Just as suddenly he stops, waits, then runs to get the cap. He feels his hair like he did before, puts the cap on his head, and makes the sign again over the cap. He squats, stroking the cap. All the others, except the* TEACHER, *leave slowly.*]

TEACHER: Victor. Sit down.

> [*Gesturing, he pats the chair.* VICTOR *comes and squats on it.*]

Good boy. Right, now. Lesson number one, let's see if you have a memory.

> [*He goes to the box and takes out three cups and an almond. He places the cups on the table. He shows* VICTOR *the almond and then places it under one of the cups. He lifts the cup several times, showing* VICTOR *that the almond is there. When he is sure that* VICTOR *is aware of the almond, he proceeds.*]

Now, Victor, watch.
  [*He moves the cups around on the table and stops when they are in a new order.*]
Victor! Where is it? Where . . . is .. it?
  [*He also signs the question. Slowly and tentatively,* VICTOR *reaches out to the cups and moves his hand to the one concealing the almond.* TEACHER *prevents him from taking the almond, but praises him lavishly.*]
Good boy. Good boy. Victor. Excellent! Now, once again.
  [*He repeats the experiment, this time faster. Again,* VICTOR *chooses the correct cup.* TEACHER *repeats the experiment, even faster and with many more moves of the cups.* VICTOR *still chooses the correct cup and finally is given the almond as a reward. He runs around the space, obviously delighted.*]
All right, that's enough. Come on. Sit down. Come on, Victor. Sit down — here!
  [VICTOR *squats on the chair, eager to play the next 'game'.*]
Now Victor, watch and listen. Who are you? You're *Victor!* That's your name. *Victor. Vic-tor.* Now you say it. *Vic-tor.* [*gesturing*] Say it.
  [VICTOR *looks up each time his name is spoken, but quickly loses interest. The* TEACHER *moves closer to him and takes hold of his hands.* TEACHER *places one hand on his own throat and the other on his lips.*]
Vic-tor. Vic-tor.
  [VICTOR *looks on, fascinated. He pats the* TEACHER'S *mouth so that the word comes out 'Vic-tor-or-or-or', then he puts his hand over his own mouth and blows through the fingers. The* TEACHER *moves away from the table.*]
Oh, dear. No good. Try again.
  [*He goes to the box and takes out a teddy bear.*]
Victor! Look! A teddy. *Victor's own teddy.*
  [*He puts it on the table and moves it towards* VICTOR, *who is terrified.*]
Come on, Victor. It's for you. Don't be afraid.
It's *Victor's* toy.

[VICTOR *turns away and clings to the back of the chair. The* TEACHER *gives up in frustration, leaving the teddy on the table.*]

Oh, dear.

[VICTOR *turns slowly and looks at the toy. He stands and reaches out to touch it. Finally he picks it up, examining it closely. He laughs gently.*]

[*coming back to him eagerly*] Yes. Yes. Victor's toy. Victor's lovely toy.

[VICTOR *suddenly rushes round the room, ripping the head, arms and legs off the toy. He throws the body at the* TEACHER, *who is furious.*]

Bad Victor. Come here. *Come here.*

[*He chases* VICTOR *and catches him.*]

I'll teach you . . . you little . . .

[VICTOR *is panic-stricken and struggles to get free.*]

Keep still, right! You've asked for it!

[*He climbs onto the table and drags* VICTOR *up with him. He holds him about the waist and if possible, lifts him out over the edge of the table.*]

See that window? See it! It's a long way down, isn't it, eh? Now shut up, or I'll drop you. Do you hear me? I'll drop you, if you don't shut up. Shut up. Stop that noise.

[VICTOR *is terrified. The* PARENT *rushes in.*]

PARENT: Is anything wrong? Oh, dear, what are you doing. What on earth are you doing? Put him down, please. What are you doing to him? He's terrified, poor thing. Fancy hanging him out of the window like that.

[VICTOR *is released by the* TEACHER, *who is most embarrassed.* VICTOR *runs straight to the* PARENT, *clutches at her dress and legs and sobs loudly.*]

There, there. Oh, dear me, what has happened, eh? There, it's all right now.

[VICTOR *calms down.*]

TEACHER: He has to learn that when he is bad, he is punished. See, he's crying.

PARENT: He doesn't even know what's good and bad. It's cruel to frighten him like that.

TEACHER: Sometimes you must be cruel to be kind. He has

to learn that he can no longer do just what he wants to. He's not in the forest any more. This is the real world. Good. Bad. Right. Wrong. Cruel. Kind.

PARENT: More bad than good. More wrong than right. And more cruel than kind. Enough is enough. Leave him alone for now.

[*The* TEACHER *goes. The* PARENT *slowly stands* VICTOR *up and gently removes his vest, shirt and trousers. She takes a blanket from the box, while* VICTOR *leaps about, free. She makes a bed on the table.*]

Come on, time for bed, Sleep.

[*She gestures sleep.* VICTOR *looks at her. She repeats the gesture 'sleep'. He comes and runs his hand over the bed. She gestures again. He coyly repeats it and leaps onto the bed. Again, he gestures sleep.*]

There, a good night's sleep and everything will be all right.

[*He leans forward and hugs her. He takes her arm and makes her come closer and sit on the bed. Then he takes her hand and draws it over his eyes, his forehead, the back of his head. He laughs and leans forward to hug her knees, rubbing them and putting his lips to them*]

Come on, Victor, lie down here and I'll tell you a story ... Once upon a time, far, far away, in the deep, dark forest where people dare not go, there lived a poor woodcutter and his wife and two children. The family had little food to eat. 'What are we going to do?' said the poor woodcutter to his wife. 'How can we feed our children when we don't even have anything for ourselves?' 'You know what,' answered the wife, 'First thing in the morning we'll take the children out into the forest, to the thickest part of all. We'll make a fire, give them each some bread and go off to our work, and leave them there alone. They won't be able to find their way back home, and we'll have got rid of them for good ...'

[*The parent stands quietly and leaves. When she has gone,* VICTOR *gets out of bed and timidly approaches the 'window'. He reaches out carefully and touches the sill, standing on tip-toe and gazing wistfully into the distance. He leans down to the box and takes out a cup and stands sipping from it as he continues to gaze out of the window.*]

VICTOR: [*slowly and deliberately*] Oh, dear. Oh, dear.
[*He repeats it, over and over. The* TEACHER *enters and stops to listen.* VICTOR *becomes aware of him and stops, afraid of him. The* TEACHER *carefully moves towards him.*]

TEACHER: Oh, dear.

VICTOR: Oh. Dear.
[*The* TEACHER *goes and gets* VICTOR's *cap and holds it out as a peace offering*]

TEACHER: Here, Victor. I'm sorry. Sorry.
[VICTOR *takes the cap.*]
Come on, young man. Let's get you dressed. We've got work to do.
[*He gets* VICTOR's *clothes and dresses him.* VICTOR *gets his cap and sits at the table. The* TEACHER *picks up the cup.*]
[*Transforming the sound of 'Oh, dear' into 'Water'*] Oh, dear. *Wa-ter.* Water.
[*He takes the cup to the table.*]
Listen, Victor. Water. [*He drinks from the cup*] Water. [*He drinks again*] Water.
[*He puts the cup on the table and gestures drinking; he points to it, then gestures.*]
Water.
[*There is no response from* VICTOR.]
Oh, dear. Come on.

VICTOR: Oh. Dear. Oh. Dear.

TEACHER: No! *Wa-ter.* [*Gesturing*] *Wa-ter.*
[VICTOR *signs 'water', points to the cup, then signs again.*]
Water. Say it. *Water.*
[VICTOR *thumps the table. Points at the cup. Signs 'water'. Thumps table.*]
Oh, dear.

VICTOR: Oh. Dear.

[*The* TEACHER *gets some water and fills the cup.* VICTOR *drinks. Signs 'water'. Laughs. Drinks. Signs 'water'. The* TEACHER *grabs the cup from him.*]

TEACHER: Water. Say it. *Water. Ask* me for it.

[VICTOR *grabs the cup back. Looks into it then dips his fingers into it and gently runs them over his lips. Then he dips them in again and runs them over the* TEACHER's *lips. Then he signs 'water'.*]

Say it. Just once. *Please.*

[*The* PARENT *enters with* VICTOR's *jacket. He runs to her.*]

PARENT: Time for your walk, Victor. Put your jacket on.

[VICTOR *puts the jacket on with some difficulty, then grabs the* PARENT *by the hand and runs out of the room with her. The* TEACHER *stays, sitting at the table. The* CHORUS *enter.*]

CHORUS: Have you heard?
The boy can say two words.
It's absurd!
The boy uses signs instead of words.
Oh dear, dear teacher, dear, oh dear.
Nothing much after one whole year.

[*They form a 'street' across the front of the performing area, bustling back and forth and occasionally stopping briefly to repeat sections of the above. The* PARENT *and* VICTOR *enter the street,* VICTOR *half-running, excited and active, like a puppy, running around her, turning somersaults, etc. The* CHORUS *carry on, ignoring his antics.*]

PARENT: What a beautiful day. The sun shining, the air so fresh. On days like this I wish the city would just melt away, so I could be back in the countryside where I come from ... Poor Victor, you must feel like that all the time —

[*During her speech,* VICTOR *has kept moving and is now physically separated from her by the* CHORUS.]

Victor? Victor!

[*She panics, running along the street, calling his name. He has also become aware of the separation and tries to find her, but is prevented from doing so by the*

CHORUS. *He finally stops, muttering 'Oh. Dear', and she finds him. She chastises him gently, greatly relieved to find him. She leads him home. He makes quiet whimpers and touches her to make sure she's really there. Once home, he crouches and rocks back and forth, staring straight ahead.*]
  . . . and I finally found him, further down the street. It was awful. When I think of what could have happened to him.

TEACHER: Well, he's home safely now, and that's all that matters. Look at him. It's certainly frightened him. He's very upset.

    [VICTOR *gets his cup and stands looking over the audience, drinking.*]

PARENT: It all seems so cruel at times. When I see him standing there, looking out the window at the hills in the distance. At the place, so far away, that was his home.

TEACHER: But today he proved that he's left it behind. He had the chance to run away, to leave all of this and go back to his forest, to the wolves who were his family. But he stayed and came back to this family. He is one of us!

CHORUS: What's this you're saying?
           What's all this fuss?
           You think the boy's finally
           Become one of us!
           A child of dark secrets
           And deep mystery
           Can never really
           Be like you and me.

TEACHER: He can walk.
PARENT: He is gentle.
TEACHER: He is clean.
PARENT: He is kind.
TEACHER: He can eat with a knife and fork.
           He wears clothes.
PARENT: He is honest.
TEACHER: He can think.
PARENT: He is good.
           He is healthy in body and mind.

CHORUS: But —
             Does he know what's good and bad?
             Does he know what's sane from mad?
             Will he ever sing a song?
             Can he tell what's right from wrong?
TEACHER: If being able to tell right from wrong is what
    makes us different from the animals, then I will prove to
    you once and for all that this boy is not an animal.
CHORUS 1: Very well, then, go ahead.
CHORUS 2: Yes, show us. We'd like to see.
CHORUS 3: We'll be the jury for his trial.
CHORUS 2: His examination.
CHORUS 1: His test.
PARENT: Please, just leave him alone. Let him live and be
    happy. Forget about your tests and leave him.
TEACHER: I'm sorry, but I have to know. I must prove that
    we have won. That we have turned a savage wolf boy into
    the real boy, Victor.
    [*Calling*] Victor!
        [VICTOR *turns and runs eagerly to the table, ready to
        start a lesson. Everybody stands back to watch. The*
        TEACHER *talks and gestures.*]
    Victor, bring me the book.
        [VICTOR *runs to the box and brings back a book. He
        gestures 'Victor brings you the book'.*]
    Good boy. Excellent.
        [VICTOR *laughs, jumps, claps his hands and shakes
        hands with the* TEACHER. *Then he sits back, ready for
        the next test.*]
    Victor, bring me my hat.
        [VICTOR *runs and rummages in the box and brings
        back the hat. He also conceals the* TEACHER*'s gloves
        behind his back, gesturing 'I bring you the hat'. He
        then presents the gloves.*]
TEACHER: Good boy. Good boy. And my gloves, too.
    Excellent!
        [VICTOR *repeats his elation. He runs, laughing, to
        shake hands with the* CHORUS *and then runs to the*
        PARENT.]

You see, he knows when he has been good. It's plain for all to see. But watch what happens now.

> [*He becomes extremely angry and severe in manner and tone of voice.* VICTOR *stops and looks at him, bewildered, shaking his head.*]

Victor, No! Bad boy. Come here. *Come here.* Right. You know what happens when you're bad. Into the cupboard. Come on.

> [*He grabs* VICTOR *by the arm and leads him towards the cupboard which has been formed by the* CHORUS *by tipping the table on end, legs facing the audience.*]

Come on, you bad boy. Into the cupboard.

> [VICTOR *goes with him right to be 'door' of the cupboard. The* TEACHER *then tries to put him inside.* VICTOR *reacts wildly and powerfully, spreading his hands and feet out to the legs of the table so that he is wedged there, with the* TEACHER *trying to push him inside. The* PARENT *is alarmed and questions what is happening, and finally struggles with the* TEACHER *in order to free* VICTOR. VICTOR *suddenly turns and attacks the* TEACHER, *hitting and biting him.* VICTOR *runs to the* PARENT.]

PARENT: Will you never learn? Will you never see how cruel you are? Now you hurt him and frighten him. You may be a teacher, but you have a lot to learn.

TEACHER: You see? He knew that I was wrong to punish him when he had done nothing wrong. He understands. He knows right from wrong. He can talk — not with words — I don't think that anyone will ever teach him that — but with signs. And in every other way he is just like you and me. He really is Victor, our great victory!

CHORUS 1: Victory

CHORUS 2: Victory

CHORUS 3: Victory

> [*On each 'victory',* VICTOR *leaps about, making victory gestures and signs. He stops. Everyone freezes with victory gestures*]

VICTOR: [*gesturing*]
            I/know/good/bad

I/know/sane/mad
I/know/right/wrong
I/know/sing/song
[*He then 'sings' the following in gesture, while the others sing the words.*]

CHORUS: If I could take you by the hand,
            Lead you far away from here,
            To a strange and different land,
            Where things are not what they appear,
            I would be the teacher there
            And you would have to learn
            That when you run, you are the wind,
            And when you climb, you are the tree,
            And when you eat and when you drink
            The food and water set you free.
            And when you eat and when you drink
            The food and water set you free.
            Could you forget who you are now
            And change into another me?

[*The* TEACHER *and the* PARENT *move to* VICTOR. *The* PARENT *takes his hand and together they turn to say farewell to the* TEACHER. *They go off in opposite directions. The three* CHORUS *break from their victory poses.*]

CHORUS: Happily ever after
            Is what the stories say.
            But is that true?
            And what do you do
            When the stories just don't end that way?
            All we can do is leave you now,
            And thank you with a perfect bow,
            It's the only civilised thing to do.
            Thank you.
            Thank you.
            And thank you, too.

THE END

Until Ya Say Ya Love Me

Magpie Theatre-in-Education Company

State Theatre Company of South Australia

Helene Burden and Maree Cochrane in the Magpie Theatre-in-Education Company production of *Until Ya Say Ya Love Me*. Photo by David Wilson.

FOREWORD

> Adolescents seem confused about what is expected of them in their relationships with the opposite sex and no wonder! Their parents can't talk about it, their peers talk about it constantly and the media are shouting 'Be in it' from every direction.
>
> *Australian Family Physician*, May, 1979

The subject matter of this play is young people and their sexuality, a guarantee of both popularity among youthful audiences and trouble from many adults. As events turned out with *Until Ya Say Ya Love Me*, Magpie was disappointed in neither direction.

Why get involved in such a minefield?

The so-called 'permissive' society sets an uncomfortable dilemma for children, their parents and educators. Sexuality is flaunted everywhere yet young Australians are still appallingly misinformed and often misled about themselves as sexual beings. Some parents are able to talk to their children about sex. Most, as the actors found out in conversations with Adelaide teenagers, are not. At the time the play was researched, forty per cent of Australian women fell pregnant before they were twenty years old and sexually transmitted diseases were on the rise among teenagers.

Knowing this was important in generating enthusiasm for a play which dealt with these matters. Important also, was the memory of each member of the company, some not all that many years removed from that critical time of growing up.

So, it was thought, just possibly the company could do some good with such a play. It would allow the audience to see their fears, their experiences, their embarrassments, dealt with in the third person. It could all be talked about in the context of what Jeff and Kerry in the play felt; how Kerry's mother reacted.

The tale is very mild and straighforward and in no way suggests that teenagers go out and experiment. It also stays within the bounds of heterosexuality. To deal with homosexuality would require a separate play. The characters in the play are faced with very common dilemmas and try to solve them with varying levels of embarrassment and success. If anything, the play says young people have to be responsible for their own actions, and to do this they must seek proper advice from parents and professional counsellors of whatever kind.

The play caused plenty of heartburn in the higher levels of the Education Department when it was first previewed, and the company was warned of the minefield ahead. Doubtless they could imagine the mountains of angry parental letters arriving on their desks in the coming months as the play made waves across the city and the provincial areas. Yet, as usual, the fears were more imagined than real. This play was one of the most successful of all Australian theatre-in-education plays.

There was controversy in some country areas where some groups objected strongly to sexual matters being discussed with children, outside the home. However, the company always ensured that teachers knew the content of the play and that when in doubt, teachers gained parental permission for the children to see the play. The performances in some places were to an audience of students and their parents and were followed by a lot of discussion. A few schools signed on for the sex-education curriculum after the play had been performed. In one town however — forever etched in the memories of the cast and crew — it really was a case of the director muttering to the stage manager 'Quick . . . start the engines . . .' as the protectors of virtue began to look exceedingly threatening.

Until Ya Say Ya Love Me is another of Magpie's group-devised and created plays. It involved all members of the company in one way or another, but it is the cast itself which deserves the ultimate applause for creating and performing the work: Marilyn Allen, Helene Burden, Maree Cochrane, Des James and Igor Sas. They created a play which did what no slide lecture or talk could do — put teenage worries and fears, problems and hopes, into flesh and blood reality.

John Lonie and Malcolm Moore, December 1984

Until Ya Say Ya Love Me was first performed by the Magpie Theatre-in-Education Company at Campbelltown High School, Adelaide, on 24 April 1980 with the following cast:

JEFF	Igor Sas
KERRY	Helene Burden
DEL CHEMIST	Marilyn Allen
KEV ALEX JACKO CHEMIST'S ASSISTANT BRIAN	Des James
BEV CHERYL	Maree Cochrane

Directed by Malcolm Moore and Des James
Designed by Richard Roberts
Stage Managed by Detlef Bauer
Research by John Lonie

CHARACTERS

JEFF, a sixteen-year-old boy
KERRY, a fifteen-year-old girl
DEL, Kerry's mother
KEV, Kerry's father
BEV, Kerry's sister
CHERYL, Kerry's friend
ALEX, Jeff's brother
JACKO, Jeff's friend
BRIAN, Bev's husband (voice only)
CHEMIST AND ASSISTANT
MALE AND FEMALE FIGURES OF FANTASY
TEACHER

SETTING

The play takes place in the homes of Jeff, Kerry, and Bev; in a chemist shop; at a party; and in the classroom.

SCENE ONE

KERRY: [*on telephone*] Hello?
JEFF: [*on telephone*] Hi.
KERRY: Hi.
JEFF: Who's that?
KERRY: Kerry.
JEFF: Hi, Kerry.
KERRY: Hi. Who's that?
JEFF: Guess.
KERRY: I don't know. Who do you want to speak to? Me?
JEFF: Yeah.
KERRY: Yeah?
   [*Pause*]
 Are you in my class?
JEFF: Nah. A year above ya.
KERRY: A year?
JEFF: Yeah.
KERRY: Mr Dempsy's form?
JEFF: That's right.
KERRY: Ah, you got blue eyes?
JEFF: Yeah.
KERRY: And hair.
JEFF: [*Laughing*] No. I'm bald.
KERRY: Oh, you know what I mean. I mean, brown hair?
JEFF: Yeah.
KERRY: Go on, tell me who you are, I don't want to guess. I might guess the wrong one. I mean . . .
JEFF: What do ya mean, the wrong one?
KERRY: Oh, you know, I might be talking to the wrong person.
JEFF: Who else has been ringin' you up?

KERRY: Oh, no one, Jeff, you know that.
JEFF: How are ya, anyway?
KERRY: Good thanks.
JEFF: Yeah?
    [*Pause.*]
  Um, er, how's that film we saw at school today?
KERRY: [*laughing*] . . . Yeah.
JEFF: Yeah. Yeah. Hey, how was it when Jacko, uh, lit up
  that cigarette?
KERRY: [*laughing*] Yeah.
JEFF: Old Dempsy went chocko.
KERRY: Yeah.
JEFF: Uh, what are you doing Saturday night?
KERRY: Oh, just babysitting for my sister, Bev.
JEFF: Oh . . .
    [*Pause.*]
KERRY; Uh, well, I'll get Mum to do it if I'm going out
  somewhere.
JEFF: Where are you going, then?
KERRY: Nowhere yet. Just babysitting.
JEFF: Oh . . .
KERRY: I mean, that's what I'm doing if there's nothing else.
JEFF: Ah, well you know Roscoe's got this party Saturday
  night. You know Roscoe?
KERRY: Yeah, course I know Roscoe.
JEFF: Yeah, well, everyone's going.
KERRY: Yeah, yeah, I heard about it.
JEFF: Do you want to go with me?
KERRY: What, to the party?
JEFF: Yeah.
KERRY: Yeah. That'll be great.
JEFF: Oh, great, um, I'll pick you up at about seven-thirty.
  Um, Jacko's taking his panel van.
KERRY: Is he?
JEFF: Yeah, and he's taking Cheryl.
KERRY: Yeah, I know, she told me. She talked about it all
  day.
JEFF: Oh, gee, is that all youse girls talk about?
KERRY: Oh, we're best friends. We're allowed to.

JEFF: Yeah, I'll pick you up about seven-thirty then.

KERRY: How we getting there?

JEFF: In Jacko's panel van.

KERRY: Oh. Then can you pick me up at the deli, then?

JEFF: Why, what's going on at the deli?

KERRY: Oh, nothing, I just got to do something there, at about seven-thirty . . . so, uh.

JEFF: Are you working there or something?

KERRY: No, I'm not working there. I just have to buy something for somebody about seven-thirty, so can you pick me up outside the deli, you know, the one on the corner.

JEFF: Why can't we pick you up at your place?

KERRY: 'Cos I'm going to be at the deli.

JEFF: All right.

KERRY: Great.

JEFF: Should be a good party.

KERRY: Oh, yeah. They usually are.

JEFF: Roscoe's last one, you know what everyone said about it?

KERRY: Yeah, I heard.

JEFF: Yeah. I'll see you then.

KERRY: Right, see you Saturday.

JEFF: Yeah.

KERRY: OK.

JEFF: Well, seeya then.

KERRY: Bye.

JEFF: Yeah, alright. . . I'll see you later, then.

KERRY: OK.

JEFF: Oh, look we'll count to three, OK?

KERRY: Yeah, OK.

JEFF: One, two, three. I'll see you.

KERRY: Right. Bye.

JEFF: Bye. See ya.

KERRY: Bye. OK. See you later.

JEFF: Bye.

SCENE TWO

DEL *and* KEV *are watching television.*

DEL: Cup of tea, Kev?

KEV: Er, I wouldn't mind.

DEL: I could make you a cup of coffee.

KEV: No, a cup of tea will be fine, thanks, luv.
　　[DEL *exits.*]

DEL: [*off*] Right. I've got some nice biscuits as well. Jam fancies.

KEV: Jam fancies. I fancy something, I can tell you.
　　[DEL *enters.*]

DEL: You just watch it.

KEV: I am and it looks great.

DEL: [*handing the tea*] Here.

KEV: Thanks, Del.

DEL: I want to talk to you, Kev.

KEV: Talk. That's going to get us a long way, isn't it?

DEL: [*laughing*] Be serious. No. It's about Kerry.

KEV: What's about Kerry?

DEL: She wants to go to a party on Saturday. You think she ought to go?

KEV: Well, I don't see any reason why not. We'll get the house to ourselves for once, watch what we want to watch, do what we want to do, eh?

DEL: Kev...

KEV: What's on tonight?

DEL: Kev. You've only got one thing on your mind. Here, have a biscuit and settle down. Now, this party. I don't know who she's going with. She hasn't said; I suppose he's from the school. I don't know where it is either. I could ask. I don't know how we are supposed to find out about these things and make arrangements or anything? I don't want to stop her going.

KEV: Stop her? Why should we stop her? Let's talk about it

tomorrow.
 [KERRY *enters.*]
KERRY: Mum?
DEL: Hello, dear. You want a cup of tea?
KERRY: No. Did you decide anything?
DEL: About the...
KERRY: Yeah, you know.
DEL: Well, we haven't discussed it yet, dear. Uh...
 Now don't be like that.
KERRY: Yeah, but you know, you got to let me go, Mum.
DEL: I know, but we've never stopped you going anywhere,
 have we?
KERRY: I know.
DEL: Well, have we?
KERRY: No. You haven't.
DEL: Right.
KEV: Where are you off to, then?
KERRY: To a party.
KEV: I just want to know where the party is.
KERRY: It's just a party. What else do you want me to tell
 you?
KEV: Who's going?
KERRY: Everybody.
KEV: Is Richard going? I like him.
KERRY: Richard, yuk.
KEV: What's wrong with Richard?
KERRY: Oh, he was a dag.
DEL: He was a bit of a dwarf, wasn't he?
KEV: He had a lot of potential, that boy.
DEL: He's six inches shorter than she is.
KEV: I really liked his hair, though.
DEL: Oh, Kev, don't be cruel. [*To* KERRY] Who are you
 going with this time, love?
KERRY: Oh, we're just all going together.
DEL: You mean, you haven't cracked onto one this time.
KERRY: Cracked on. Oh, Mum, don't talk like that. Jeff's
 asked me.
DEL: Jeff, right, Jeff, so now we know. Is he the nice one with
 the brown hair and the blue eyes?

[KERRY *indicates that he is*.]
Quite fancy that one myself.
KEV: Eh. Take it easy.
DEL: Oh, all right. Are the parents going to be there?
KERRY: Probably.
KEV: What do you mean, 'probably'?
KERRY: I don't know. I didn't ask.
DEL: Where is it?
KERRY: At Roscoe's place.
KEV: Roscoe who?
KERRY: I don't know. That's his name. Roscoe.
KEV: Yeah, but what's his real name, what's his parents' name?
KERRY: Roscoe.
KEV: Well, they're not Mr and Mrs Roscoe.
KERRY: Yes, they are.
KEV: Roscoe, the grocers?
KERRY: Yeah, and they call him Roscoe at school.
KEV: Roscoe, right. [*To* DEL] Got the shop on Fullarton Road.
DEL: Oh, yes.
KERRY: What does it matter what they do?
DEL: Now, Kerry.
KERRY: Can I go to the party? Please?
     [*Silence*.]
It's just an ordinary party.
KEV: Well, how about telling us what time you'll be getting home.
KERRY: Oh, yeah, well . . . well, what time do I have to be in?
KEV: You tell me.
KERRY: I don't know.
KEV: Eleven-thirty.
KERRY: Eleven-thirty! It's Saturday night, Dad, nobody goes home at eleven-thirty.
DEL: How are you going to get home?
KERRY: I'll get a lift.
DEL: Are you certain of getting a lift?
KERRY: Yes, I'm certain, Jeff said.

KEV: Who're you getting a lift with?

KERRY: His friend.

KEV: Who's his friend?

KERRY: Jacko.

KEV: You mean the one with the panel van?

KERRY: Oh, there's four of us. Jacko is going with Cheryl. I'm going with Jeff. There's four of us.

KEV: Four of you in a panel van?

KERRY: We're just going to be driven home, Dad. You want me to be driven home, don't you?

DEL: Your Dad will pick you up.

KEV: What do you mean, I'll pick her up?

KERRY: [*almost simultaneously*] Oh, not Dad. It's not a kids' party. He can't pick me up.

KEV: What time can you get a lift home?

KERRY: Twelve o'clock. Oh, come on, twelve please, I can't go home at eleven-thirty. Twelve o'clock then?

DEL: Or your Dad picks you up.

KERRY: OK, well, I'll be in by twelve then.

[KERRY *exits* DEL *turns the T.V. down.*]

KEV: Well, that's sorted out.

DEL: I don't like the idea of this panel van, Kev. You should've said you'd bring her home.

KEV: Why didn't you say it before? You're her mother. Why land everything in my lap?

DEL: I did say. Anyway, you've got the car. It's your job to see she gets home safely.

KEV: What's that got to do with anything? It's not my job to be the bloody taxi-driver. I've got better things to do with my time.

DEL: You don't have to talk like that, Kev, she's your responsibility as well. I mean, she's your daughter as well as she's mine.

KEV: Don't think I don't care about her.

DEL: Well, why don't you bring her home then?

KEV: When do I get any time for myself? When do we get a chance to be on our own together, without having to leap up every five minutes to get some kid from a dance or other. When do we get a chance just to go to bed — when do we get a chance to do that, eh?

DEL: We get plenty of chances. But this is important.

KEV: There's always something bloody important, more important than me.

[*Silence.*]

DEL: [*holding out jam fancies*] Can I get you another cup of tea?

KEV: No. I'm going to bed.

[DEL *turns the T.V. off.*]

DEL: [*reminiscing*] He's right, you know. For twenty-five years there's always been something. Midnight sessions at the sewing machine, because some tearful child forgot to tell you he had to have something red to wear for Sports Day. Some ding-dong battle over who has the car to go to the drive-in. Some crisis over what someone could or could not wear to a matric dance, leading to a row between Kev and me that kept us not talking for days, or touching. Sometimes I wish I were a kid again, up at the drive-in with Kev, I think it was Kev. Pretending to watch Doris Day up on the silver screen holding off Frank Sinatra much more successfully than I was Kev down in the dark of the Holden. Doris Day. So jolly clean and neat we were. Three starched petticoats under the circle skirt, stiff enough to keep out any straying fingers. Persuading Mum to buy me a circle stitched bra that gave you bosoms more pointy than anything Wonder Woman ever dream-ed of. Obscene, they were, when you think about it. They made Playtex Cross-your-hearts look like body bras. And straps so tight, Kev's fumbling fingers never did manage to undo the fastener in the dark, not without help, that is. Then, back at the house, heavy breathing behind the chook house, not too heavy, not to wake the chooks, or my dad. Crikey, there he'd be, lurking on the veranda, trigger-finger at the ready to switch the outside light on any would-be Romeos. Those were the days. Kev still gets excited at the sight of suspenders. They were good days, though, because we knew where we were. We had rules. I was expected to say no to Kev, and I did. My dad would have belted me if I didn't, and Kev would've been frightened out of his life if I had. In a way the decision wasn't mine to make. It's different now, though, different game, different rules. Decisions to be made all the time. It's no wonder I get tired, tired of watching my friends at the bowling, trying to find out what demands they make of their kids, what they let their sons do, their daughters wear, where they let them go, who with, what time they've got to get home. Tired of telephoning the mothers' mafia, checking up on other peoples' parties, so I can come to some fair decision to keep my Kerry safe and happy. You'd think after three kids and twenty-five years I'd know by now. I suppose I'm old — Kerry calls me an 'oldie', she does — I've heard her, on the phone. I don't mind — well, I do really. It's funny, though. I still see myself as the kid, back of the back veranda.

SCENE THREE

KERRY *and* CHERYL *sit at their school desks, one behind the other.*

CHERYL: Pssst! Kerry!
KERRY: What? What? Oh, I'm up to number four, Mrs Churney. Yeah. I'm just doing the maps and the gulf streams ... yes, Mrs Churney.
　　[*Footsteps are heard.*]
CHERYL: What about Saturday night, Roscoe's party, eh? ... Really looking forward to that.
KERRY: Yeah, so am I.
CHERYL: Last year, I went to one of Roscoe's parties, it was a real rage.
KERRY: Yeah
CHERYL: The guys got hold of all this beer and they got really drunk and they were jumping all over the furniture and then we started sipping the blackberry nip and the creme-de-menthe from his parents' booze cupboard. And Robyn, you know Robyn, started acting really drunk

and then all the guys threw her into the pool, then jumped in after her with all their clothes on. It was really funny.

   [*She laughs.*]

KERRY: Yeah, it sounds great.

CHERYL: You going with anyone?

KERRY: Jeff's asked me.

CHERYL: Jeff? Great, so what's this, the fifth time?

KERRY: Fourth.

CHERYL: Fourth time.

KERRY: Uh. Huh.

CHERYL: Good eh? Sh. Well, what happened last time?

KERRY: [*checking to see if the* TEACHER *is looking*] Look, I got to do this, Cheryl.

CHERYL: You can do that really quick, don't worry about it. What are you going to wear on Saturday night?

KERRY: [*getting out a magazine*] Have a look at this cigarette skirt. What do you think?

CHERYL: Have you got one?

KERRY: Mum said she'd make me one. But no slits up the sides, though. She can't stand them.

CHERYL: Yeah. Same as my mum. Really old-fashioned.

KERRY: What about my hair, though? I'm sick of my hair. I want to do something with it. I don't like it like it is.

   [CHERYL *gets up and walks to* KERRY's *desk*]

CHERYL: Well, look at those gorgeous slides. You could pin it up there, like that.

KERRY: Can I borrow your curling wand, or are you going to use it that night?

CHERYL: No. I'm not going to use if. You can have it.

KERRY: I can flick my hair off my face, like that chick in, you know, *Cleo*, last month. Remember?

CHERYL: On the front cover?

KERRY: Yeah, I want to see if I can do my eyes up like that too. See how that chick's got her eye make-up and it goes out like that.

CHERYL: Yeah, I don't like the colour, though.

KERRY: It's a nice colour, it'd suit me.

CHERYL: Yeah, could be all right if it was a bit darker, I

suppose.
KERRY: Oh, I'd look like a real slut then.
CHERYL: I wear dark eyeshadow. Are you sayin' I'm a slut?
KERRY: No. It's just that I wouldn't wear it that dark. What are you going to wear?
CHERYL: I'm going to wear my pink satin pants, and that black top, that Jacko really likes.
KERRY: The lacy one?
CHERYL: Mmm. Yeah.
KERRY: That shows your boobs?
CHERYL: Oh, it doesn't show them.
KERRY: It shows the tops of them.
CHERYL: Well, there's nothing wrong with that.
KERRY: Yeah, I know there isn't. Jacko's already seen them, anyway.

> [They laugh. The TEACHER *re-enters and walks over to the girls.*]

CHERYL: I'm just helping Kerry, Mrs Churney . . . All right!
> [*She returns to her seat. The* TEACHER *leaves.*]
How is it going with Jeff? Have you got anywhere yet?
KERRY: Shut up, the other kids might hear. What do you mean, got anywhere?
CHERYL: Well, I mean, is it still just, um. . .
KERRY: Well, we talk a bit.
CHERYL: You talk a bit. Well, that's great. . .
KERRY: Well, I don't suppose you and Jacko talk much, do you? I bet you do other things, I mean you don't exactly sit in the panel van and talk, do you?
CHERYL: Um, some of the time we do. Not all the time, though.
KERRY: How is it going with you and Jacko?
CHERYL: Oh, really well. I mean, you know what Jacko's like.
KERRY: Yeah, what's been happening?
CHERYL: Well, actually it's getting really serious now.
KERRY: Yeah?
CHERYL: He told me he loved me last week.
KERRY: Yeah, where were you?
CHERYL: In the panel van.

KERRY: In the back?

CHERYL: Yes.

KERRY: Yeah, oh.

CHERYL: What do you mean — yeah, oh? What's wrong with that?

KERRY: Nothing.

CHERYL: Anyway, it's the only private place we've got. Where else is he going to tell me he loves me?

KERRY: Yeah. . .

CHERYL: And I love him anyway.

KERRY: Yeah, I suppose you've been going out with him for four. . .

CHERYL: I think it's nearly. . .

KERRY: Oh, four and a half.

CHERYL: Yeah, it'll be five weeks on Roscoe's party.

KERRY: Yeah, that's quite a bit.

CHERYL: I mean, that's the only reason that I . . . you know . . . Went the whole way.

KERRY: Yeah, I know. What was it like?

CHERYL: OK. Great. I wouldn't have done it unless he said he loved me. It was really good.

KERRY: I don't know what I'd do if Jeffrey said that to me. I don't know what I'd do.

CHERYL: Well, why not? I mean, as long as he loves you it's all right.

KERRY: Yeah, but I don't know whether to believe him.

CHERYL: Oh, look, here comes Mrs Churney. Psst! You got to do it anyway, or you'll lose Jeff.

KERRY: I won't.

CHERYL: You will, he won't keep going out with you unless you do it.

KERRY: He likes me.

CHERYL: I know he likes you, but how long do you think he's going to keep going out with you if you don't do anything?

KERRY: We do do things.

CHERYL: Oh, what?

KERRY: Oh shut up, you don't know anything. I've got to get on with my gulf streams, so you just get on with your work.

CHERYL: You're a bloody dag.
  [*Exit* KERRY *and* CHERYL.]

SCENE FOUR

JEFF *Enters wearing jocks and towel. Music up.* JEFF *dances and does classic macho things like flexing his muscles before the mirror. Then he checks his face, squeezing the odd pimple. Then slicks back his hair and slips a pair of rolled up socks down the front of his jocks. Fade into fantasy music.*

JEFF: [*fantasising*] It's going to be a great party. I wonder what she's wearing. I can just see her now. I can see it, I can feel it. She's gonna be waiting for me, outside her apartment. Tall, blonde, big tits. Really long legs, right up to her armpits, with really high shoes. One of them real clingy outfits. I'll just walk up to her real cool and I'll just stand there and she'll look me up and down. But I'll ignore her, just for a little while. I'll pull out two cigarettes. Light them together. Give one to her, and I'll say, real cool-like. Hi!
  [*Enter* HER.]
HER: Hi, big boy.
JEFF: Then I'll just move on — no, she moves all over me. She's dying for it, she really wants it, she's so hot. But I'll just stick out the arm. We move on down the street, and some punk will come running up, and I'll say, 'Hey, cool it, creep'. She'll love me for it. She knows I'm tough.
HER: Gee, you're real tough.
JEFF: Hey, watch the threads. We slide up to the restaurant and the doorman says:
DOORMAN: Good evening, Jeff.
JEFF: Hi, Harry, don't bother me.
DOORMAN: Your table, sir.
JEFF: For two!
  [*They cuddle.*]
What do you want to drink, babe?

HER: You order for me, Big Boy.

JEFF: Harry. One blue lagoon for the lady, and I'll have a dry martini. Stirred not shaken, and don't forget the olive. She's so hot. She's dying for it. She's desperate. Drink?

HER: Take me.

  [WAITER *brings drinks.*]

JEFF: Here?

HER: Yes. Now.

JEFF: The boys are watching. Hey, rack off fellas, this is private. I mean, I don't even have to do anything, she's laying there, and I got on top.

HER: Take me away, take me away.

JEFF: She's begging me. And I climb aboard and give it to her.

HER: Best I've ever had.

JEFF: I know, it's going to be a great party.

  [*Exit* JEFF *and* HER.]

SCENE FIVE

Cheryl *and* MALE FANTASY FIGURE *enter. He addresses her via voice over. Two 'fast' women stand nearby.*

HIM: [*v/o*] You're the most beautiful woman I've ever seen.

CHERYL: [*fantasising*] Thank you. [*Pointing to the women*] What about them?

HIM: [*v/o*] Who?

CHERYL: But you've got a reputation with women.

HIM: [*v/o*] That's all in the past. I've met you. I want you.

CHERYL: Me or my body?

HIM: [*v/o*] All of you. I want you for ever.

CHERYL: I'm not like those other women. I believe in waiting.

HIM: [*v/o*] I don't care, I'll wait for ever. Can I hold you?

CHERYL: If you must.

HIM: [*v/o*] Your fingers, your wrist, your arms, your

shoulders, your neck, your hair, your perfume.

CHERYL: I saw a girl friend of mine, from school, I waved. I couldn't wait to get back to school on Monday to tell her.

HIM: [*v/o*] Please, please say you'll have me, I need you, I can't live without you.

CHERYL: We hardly know each other.

HIM: [*v/o*] We've got the rest of our lives to get to know one another, but if you want, I'll wait.

CHERYL: Yes. That's what I want.

HIM: [*v/o*] Can I see you till then? Can I take you out to dinner tomorrow? Please say yes.

CHERYL: I'd like that.

HIM: [*v/o*]May I kiss you?

CHERYL: Maybe tomorrow.

    [*She starts to move off.*]

HIM: [*v/o*] Can I have your phone number?

CHERYL: It's in the book.

SCENE SIX

KERRY *enters.* JEFF *walks in and poses.*

JEFF: Hi!

KERRY: Hi!

JEFF: Cigarette?

KERRY: I don't smoke.

JEFF: Oh, that's right. I forgot.

KERRY: Where's ya car?

JEFF: Eh, I haven't got one. Jacko's...

KERRY: Oh, yeah. I didn't mean ... Oh!

JEFF: Oh, ah, let's go then.

KERRY: All right.

    KERRY *and* JEFF *arrive at the party [party music and FX.] They greet people and start dancing together. Eventually, they hold hands and holding hands becomes kissing which becomes hugging which becomes heavy petting and fondling until* KERRY *pushes* JEFF *away.* JEFF *freezes for* KERRY's *soliloquy.*

KERRY: [*panting and excited*] Oh, jeez, I nearly got carried away then. He really knows what he's doing. I loved it when he held me really close. I didn't realise how hard it would be to stop. But I had to. Stop him, I mean. He was getting all panty and I thought he'd suffocate me with his kisses. And when he put his hand down there I really freaked. But ... after a while I sort of got horny. You know what I mean. I knew he was going to say something then. But I was sort of just hoping that it'd all be OK and he'd just be satisfied with a bit of pashing and carrying on. I mean, it's not as if I love him or anything. Jeez, if I loved him and he ... But I never even know if I'm going to see him again. He hasn't asked me to go with him or anything. I'd say yes if he did, 'cos I really like him. And then after a few weeks, I suppose it's all right to, you know, do it. But if I did do it, everyone'd get to know and all the guys will think they can get me too and even if they don't my girl friends'll think I'm a gangy and won't want to know me. And then, what if I got pregnant? My mum would just die, I know she would. And Dad would never speak to me again. I suppose I'd have to go and live with my sister, Bev. I wonder if you can get pregnant the first time? Maybe it'd be all right to do it just once ... But then Jeff might drop me 'cos he's got it out of me. Probably tell all his mates, too. But if I keep on saying no, he might get really sick of me and find someone else. I know he thinks Cheryl's pretty spunky. She'd probably give it to him. It's not fair! What if I talked to him about it? I mean, if he understood what I feel about it, what I have to go through, then it might be all right. I just don't know what to do.

[*She sits thinking.*]

JEFF: [*soliloquising*] I don't really want to do it because I'm scared. I mean, I'm horny, who wouldn't be, hell, check the dress and she's let me touch her, right, but I don't really know where to put it, you know what I mean. I mean, who tells ya these things? The folks don't tell you nothing and sex education classes don't actually tell ya how to do it. Who do ya ask? Ya mates? Christ, you'd never live it down! I'm supposed to know what to do just because I'm a guy. How stupid is that? Yeah, and I'm supposed to make it with a chick the first time I take her out. Fumble, fumble, fumble, hot breath on my neck, tit in hand and stop and what next? 'Until Ya Say Ya Love Me'? What if I just like her as a friend. Just want to talk or something. If ya don't do nothing and ya mates find out, you're slow, a dickhead. I'm almost seventeen. I don't wanna be a virgin all my life. What if it never happens? What if I never get it, who's gonna want me then? Ah, I gotta go for it, she's a chick, she'll know what to do. I've got nothing to lose.

    [*Pause.*]

Well, do you wanna do it?

KERRY: What?

JEFF: You know, let's do it.

KERRY: I don't know what you're talking about.

JEFF: You know.

KERRY: No.

JEFF: Why not?

KERRY: Well, because I don't want to.

JEFF: Oh, come on.

KERRY: Well, have you got something?

JEFF: Eh!

KERRY: Oh, you know, what if I got pregnant?

JEFF: You won't get pregnant.

KERRY: Oh, how do you know?

JEFF: Well . . . you won't. Oh come on . . . I really like ya.

KERRY: Do you?

JEFF: Yeah, course. I do.

KERRY: Do you really like me?

JEFF: Sure do. So come on, let's do it.

KERRY: Oh, it's just that I don't want to. Not yet. It's not that I don't like you, 'cos I do. . .

JEFF: Well, what's the matter then?

KERRY: Ya gotta use something.

JEFF: I'll be careful. I know how to do it.

KERRY: No!

JEFF: Well, why not, you've been leading me on all night.

KERRY: What do you mean? I haven't.

JEFF: Yeah, ya have. You let me touch you and everything.

KERRY: So what, everyone does that, it doesn't mean...

JEFF: I thought ya wanted it!

KERRY: I never said anything like that.

JEFF: Yeah, you did, you said you'd go with me to this party and I bought the drinks and everything.

KERRY: I thought you liked me just for myself.

JEFF: I do... Oh, come on, it won't hurt a bit.

KERRY: No.

JEFF: Come on!

KERRY: No — you guys don't understand.

    [*Exit* KERRY.]

JEFF: You're just frigid ... Kerry?

    [*Enter* JACKO.]

JACKO: G'day, Jeff, wondered where you was hiding. [*Confidentially*] Wanna blow a number?

JEFF: [*ill at ease*] You got a number?

JACKO: Yeah, mate, Queensland Gold. Good stuff, eh?

JEFF: [*attempting enthusiasm*] Yeah, Queensland Gold.

JACKO: Get something good, spread it around, y'know. Share it with y'mates. Guys gotta stick together, eh?

    [*He offers* JEFF *a joint.*]

JEFF: [*lost*] Yeah.

    [*But he does not take it.*]

JACKO: One of the boys, eh, Jeff?

    [*He thrusts the joint under* JEFF's *nose.*]

JEFF: Yeah?

    [*He takes the joint reluctantly.*]

  Yeah, thanks.

JACKO: [*dangling his car keys*] I saw you giving her a bit of tit. Reckoned you might be ready. [*Laughing obscenely*] Youse can warm the van up for us.

    [*He dangles the keys.*]

JEFF: What about you and Cheryl, mate?

JACKO: Don't worry about Cheryl. She'll keep. [*Jingling the keys again*] I saw you. Split her, seam to seam. Hot little tart, I reckon.

JEFF: No, don't worry about it, mate.

JACKO: Come on mate, it's better in the van. [*Becoming ugly*] I got it all fixed up.

JEFF: No, honest, Jacko, it's cool, we don't want to.

JACKO: Wassa matter, mate? Not good enough for you?

JEFF: No, she don't want to.

JACKO: [*shouting with laughter*] You gonna let that stop you?

JEFF: [*getting angry*] No. We had a fight.

JACKO: Letting a chick argue with you. Little Jeffy couldn't get it up, eh?

JEFF: Yeah, no. She gave me some crap about getting pregnant.

JACKO: They all pull that one, mate. Just playing hard to get. Never happens the first time. You know that!

JEFF: [*talking the cue*] Yeah?

JACKO: Yeah.

JEFF: Yeah, that's what I said. [*Laughing tentatively*] You know, she wanted me to use a franger.

JACKO: A franger! Hey! What sort of poof she think you are? No bloke in his right mind'd wear one of them. Like wearing a raincoat in a shower.

JEFF: Yeah?

JACKO: Yeah.

JEFF: Yeah, that's what I said.

JACKO: You got to get her worked up, man. Then ya lay it on her, she either does it or she goes.

JEFF: Yeah. What if . . . if she gets pregnant?

JACKO: Well, then you'd marry her.

JEFF: [*surprised*] Yeah. Hey, or she could have an abortion.

JACKO: Abortion! That's murder, man. That's a bit of your life in there. You got to stick by it.

JEFF: Yeah, but Jacko . . . we've only been going a few weeks. I don't fix on marrying her or nothing.

JACKO: That's easy then. Kick her in the guts. No problem. [JEFF *stares at him uncomprehendingly.* JACKO *goes off on his own imagination kick.*] I'll do it for you. Anything for a mate. [*Laughing*] Get the boys down. She'll never know whose it is. Then we'll all

kick her in the guts. No problems. Ya coming?
JEFF: Yeah!
      [JACKO *and* JEFF *exit.*]

SCENE SEVEN

Enter KERRY *and* BEV.

KERRY: You wearing that dress to the dinner tonight?
BEV: Oh, it'll do, I think. Oh, does my hair look all right? I
    just didn't have time to wash it today.
KERRY: Yeah, it's really nice.
BEV: How are you going, anyway?
KERRY: Well...
BEV: I'll just sit down here and put my face on. Will you be
    all right tonight, looking after the baby?
KERRY: Yeah, sure...
BEV: Now, you know where his feed is? You know where the
    nappies are? You know if he cries, don't go picking him
    up.
KERRY: Why not? I like to.
BEV: No, just ignore him.
BRIAN: [*off*] Come on, hurry up. We're late.
KERRY: Brian's calling.
BEV: Ignore him, too. How are you? You've hardly said a
    word since you've been here.
KERRY: I'm OK. I wanted to talk to you.
BEV: Oh, OK. Are you going to have anyone around
    tonight? How about this new Jeff fella? Mum told me you
    went out with him on Saturday.
KERRY: Think it was the last time.
BEV: I thought it was the first time.
KERRY: Oh, no. We've been going out for a couple of weeks,
    something like that...
BEV: Oh, look at that bloody ladder in my stockings.
BRIAN: [*off*] Bev.

BEV: Oh, for God's sake, be quiet.

BRIAN: [*off*] Where is my shirt?

BEV: What?

BRIAN: [*off*] Have you ironed my shirt?

BEV: Oh, I've got to do everything. These will have to do.

KERRY: Bev, did you and Brian do it before you got married?

BEV: What? Oh well, what on earth do you want to know that for?

KERRY: Oh, I just wondered. I don't know what to do with Jeff, that's all.

BEV: You don't know what to do with him? But you just said you're not going to see him again anyway.

KERRY: I know, because we had a bit of a hassle on Saturday night at the party. That's what I wanted to talk about. Well, he's a bit older than me. Oh, he wanted to do it and I didn't, you know? I don't know what I wanted.

BEV: Was he trying to make you do it?

KERRY: Sort of.

BEV: Do you like him? Do you want to do it?

KERRY: Yeah, I like him, and if I see him again, I don't know whether I could say no next time.

BEV: Well, you've just got to make up your own mind. But just make sure it's your own decision.

BRIAN: [*off*] I still can't find me shirt.

BEV: [*yelling*] Well, bloody well look for it yourself!

KERRY: You see, Bev, I haven't got a boyfriend. I'd like him as a boyfriend.

BEV: You can't do it with somebody just because you want a boyfriend, Kerry. Why do you have to go to bed with each other?

KERRY: Because. You can't have a good time or keep a boy-friend unless you do it. And if I got pregnant, I could get an abortion.

BEV: Abortion?

KERRY: Just joking.

BEV: There's no need for it to go that far. Look, if you're going to do it with the guy, either you've got to go on the pill, or he's got to use something. Now, have you thought about that?

KERRY: Yeah. I know all about that.

BEV: Well, why don't you do something?

KERRY: I can't go on the pill. I'm too young. Everyone'll think I'm slack.

BEV: Why does everyone have to know? Well, if you don't want to go on the pill yet, have you or Jeff thought about using condoms? They're so cheap and so easy to get. Kerry, don't be dumb. You could get pregnant, for God's sake. You only have to do it once.

KERRY: He'll be careful. We'll be all right.

BEV: Look, you're asking for my advice. If you get stuck with a baby at fifteen, it'll change your life. You won't be able to go out to discos and parties as much. Do you think the boys are going to ask you out when you've got a screaming brat to look after? It'll make you a woman, Kerry. That's how the kids will look at you, not as one of them any more. Kerry, you have to use precautions. Either you go on the pill, or Jeff uses a condom, or you go and buy some. But if you want to go on the pill, you'll have to talk to Mum about it.

KERRY: I can't talk to Mum.

BEV: You have to. Come on, this isn't a little girls game you're playing. You're making an adult decision. If you're old enough to make the decision, then you're old enough to go and face Mum. And if not, you'll have to talk to Jeff about it.

BRIAN: [*off*] Will someone come and help me iron me shirt?
     [*Exit* KERRY.]

BEV: [*soliloquising*] Oh, that stupid bloody kid. I've heard it all before. 'I won't get pregnant, he'll be careful, it'll be all right.' If only it was. I said exactly the same thing ten years ago. Look at me now. Married, two kids, same old routine. When I think how it could have been if I hadn't got pregnant. You wouldn't have known me then. Long blonde hair, good figure, tight jeans, long days on the beach in a tiny bikini, sunbaking, swimming, not a care in the world, no responsibilities, no one to please but ourselves. We used to go to a party or a dance every Saturday night. Pam and I would spend all Saturday afternoon getting ready. We would have long bubble baths and my poor father would scream and curse when he wanted to use the bathroom. Then we would go through our entire wardrobe trying everything on and then still insist that we had nothing to wear and I would beg my mother to make me a new dress or buy me yet another pair of jeans. I used to take an hour to blow-dry my hair and another hour doing my make-up. Looking back now, the parties and the dances were never as much fun as the preparation. Pam and I would talk and dream about the future. I always thought I would do well at school. Be the only one in our family to go to uni . . . I would meet an older man there, just finishing Medicine or Law. He would be handsome and strong and fall immediately in love with me. Church wedding, big reception and then he would whisk me away. We would return to a beautiful house. [*Stopping, looking round*] Not like this. I never dreamt it would be like this. I wouldn't have married Brian. I had to, I had no choice. But now, it's so easy to plan everything. The girls can go on the pill, it's not as if it's hard to get. Kids, they worry about their parents finding out. It's a lot easier to face your mother with that rather than having to tell her you're pregnant. I ought to know. I'll never forget Mum's face, how disappointed she was. And Dad!

[*Exit* BEV.]

SCENE EIGHT

Enter JEFF.

JEFF: Where's my socks? Don't worry about it. I'll get a pair from Alex. Bloody woman, ought to be locked up. Drop ya daks, turn ya back and they're in the wash.
[*He rummages through the drawers and finds some condoms.*]

Hell!

    [*Enter* ALEX.]

ALEX: [*throwing down his sandshoes*] Bloody mongrel waste of time. What were you doing in my cupboard?

JEFF: [*guiltily*] Just borrowing some socks.

ALEX: Why weren't you at practice?

JEFF: Give it a miss.

ALEX: Should have given it a miss as well.

JEFF: Why?

ALEX: The oval's ploughed up.

JEFF: What?

ALEX: That wanker Jacko — as if you didn't know.

JEFF: Me?

ALEX: Yeah, you. You went to that party last night, didn't ya?

JEFF: Yeah, I did, but what's that got to do with it?

ALEX: In the panel van?

JEFF: So?

ALEX: So it was seen ripping up the oval — as if you didn't know. You and Jacko. Bum buddies till the end. He even had the cheek to hang about this arvo and gloat about your handiwork.

JEFF: Listen, Jacko's not me mate. I wasn't with him last night.

ALEX: Bullshit. I saw him pick you up. Met some moll, didn't you? Spent the night shagging on the oval.

JEFF: She's not a moll. We didn't do nothing.

ALEX: Yeah, all right, I got to get ready. I'm going out.

JEFF: Look, Kerry's a good chick, OK. We left early and I took a bus home.

ALEX: You didn't take her home?

JEFF: No.

ALEX: You didn't make it?

JEFF: No. We had a fight.

ALEX: Yeah?

JEFF: Yeah. Gave me some crap about getting pregnant. We were going great guns. She let me touch her and everything and then she said no.

ALEX: Yeah. Well, it's easy to get pregnant.

JEFF: Bullshit. Not the first time, Jacko told me that.

ALEX: Stuff Jacko. That cretin hasn't got a brain in his head. A chick can get pregnant any time. Any time, mate.

JEFF: Yeah, I know that.

ALEX: Look, I gotta go. Joanne's waiting for me. [*Rummaging through the drawers*] Where's me bloody wet checks?

JEFF: You mean these?

ALEX: What are you doing with them? Oh, I see. You and Kerry?

JEFF: No way, mate, I wouldn't be caught dead with those. Jacko says it's like wearing a raincoat in a shower. Alex?

ALEX: Yeah, mate.

JEFF: Do you and Joanne use those things?

ALEX: Mad not to. You don't want a kid on ya hands, do you?

JEFF: No!

ALEX: I've gotta go. Look, I need these. If you want some why don't you try the Shell garage down the road, or why don't you try the chemist?

[*Exit* ALEX. JEFF, *worried and nervous, walks to and fro. Enter* CHEMIST.]

CHEMIST: Yes, can I help you?

JEFF: Ah, yes.

CHEMIST: Yes, what?

JEFF: Yes, please.

CHEMIST: No, do you want to buy something?

JEFF: Yeah, I ah . . .

CHEMIST: Yes, yes . . . yes

JEFF: Um, ah, I ah, wanna.

CHEMIST: Look, you're not ethnic, are you?

JEFF: What?

CHEMIST: I said, oh, never mind . . . Are you deaf? I said [*shouting*] *Are — you — deaf?*

JEFF: No!

CHEMIST: Well, then, out with it, boy. Come on, come on, I haven't got all day . . . What's the matter? Cat got your tongue? Locked in the linguistic lobes, short circuit between the earphones, eh?

JEFF: Sorry?

CHEMIST: *What — do — you — want?*

JEFF: [*shouting back*] I'd like a fran, fra, fr, fra, a . . . froat lozenge, thanks.

CHEMIST: One or two?

JEFF: What?

CHEMIST: We don't sell them individually, you know. One packet or two?

JEFF: Oh, um, one packet, thanks.

CHEMIST: Five dollars, thank you.

JEFF: Five bucks, Geez, what size is that for?

CHEMIST: I beg your pardon?

JEFF: Er, do they come in different sizes?

CHEMIST: Different sizes — lozenges — no, they don't come in different sizes. Anyone would think you want to buy a condom.

JEFF: No! . . . Ah.

CHEMIST: That's it, isn't it? You want to buy a condom. [*Grabbing a megaphone*] Attention! Attention everyone!
    [*Enter* ASSISTANT.]
This boy, yes, this boy going red right here, this filthy degenerate, immoral, perverted little boy wants to buy a condom. C-O-N-D-O-M. What does that spell?

JEFF: Condom.

CHEMIST: Again.

JEFF: Condom.

CHEMIST: Louder.

JEFF: Condom.

CHEMIST: Yes, a rubber, French letter, franger, sleeping bag for mice, Durex, and I don't mean tape. What size is it?
    [ASSISTANT, *with tape measure and magnifying glass, grabs* JEFF.]

JEFF: Size, please, no.

CHEMIST: Yes. Is it large, is it medium? Small? Tiny? Miniature? MICROSCOPIC?

JEFF: Help! Ah!

CHEMIST: Roll up, roll up, ladies and gentlemen! Come and

see a wonder never revealed before white eyes, a sight so
devastating it makes grown men weep. The world's
smallest . . .

    [JEFF *runs off. Pause.* JEFF *re-enters.*]

CHEMIST: Yes, can I help you?

JEFF: Yeah, I'd like a . . . I'd like a packet of condoms,
  please.

CHEMIST: Wetchex be sufficient?

JEFF: Yes, a packet of three, please.

    Ah, do you wanna know the size?

CHEMIST: Oh, they're all the same size. That's seventy-nine
  cents, thank you.

JEFF: Thank you. 'Bye.

CHEMIST: Have a nice day.

JEFF: Uh, yeah, thanks.

    [*Exit* JEFF *and* CHEMIST.]

SCENE NINE

Enter DEL *and* BEV.

BEV: Mum.

DEL: Hello, Bev dear. How are you, love?

BEV: I've just put Bradley in the lounge, he's asleep. What
  are you doing?

DEL: Oh, making a stew for dinner tonight.

BEV: Mmm, smells good.

DEL: All the best stuff here, Mum and Margaret Fulton.

BEV: Can I make you a cup of tea?

DEL: No, thanks, and to what do we owe this pleasure?

BEV: I just thought I'd drop in and see if Kerry would baby-
  sit again for me this week-end.

DEL: Oh, yes, I'm sure she will.

BEV: She's not going out?

DEL: No, I don't think so. Is that all you came for? You
  could have rung up about that.

BEV: Oh, no, I just thought I'd pop in. She came over the

other night, and we had a bit of a chat about things, you know.

DEL: Oh, yeah, she's been a bit quiet this week.

BEV: Has she? Has she talked to you about this Jeff boy she's been going out with at all?

DEL: No. Should she have? He seems a nice enough boy to me.

BEV: I was a bit worried about her this week. She seemed a bit different from normal, not her usual happy-go-lucky self.

DEL: What do you mean, Bev?

BEV: Well, I think she's quite worried about this relationship with Jeff. Hasn't she said anything?

DEL: They're only kids. I can't see that they've got anything worry about. Either she likes him or she doesn't like him.

BEV: Well, I think it's a bit more serious than that.

DEL: Well, what's she been saying to you, then?

BEV: Well, she came to me for advice.

DEL: Why didn't she come to me for advice? I'm her mother.

BEV: Well, I don't know, she came to me, didn't she? And she's upset and she's worried about all this. She wants to see Jeff again.

DEL: Well, there's nothing preventing her from seeing Jeff. She can go and see him any time she wants. She's going to a party this week. She can go with him if he wants to go with her. I mean, nobody is stopping her. Is that what she's saying, that we are stopping her going out with Jeff?

BEV: No. Now just settle down, all right.

DEL: Well, you seem to be accusing me of . . .

BEV: Maybe you've just forgotten. I mean, when I started going out with Brian, it didn't take all that long for us to get around to . . . Look, kids these days are doing things a lot younger than when I was at school.

DEL: What do you mean, doing things? I'm sure Kerry wouldn't do anything like that.

BEV: Well, I don't really think she does, just yet . . .

    [KERRY *enters.*]

KERRY: What are you talking about?

DEL: Oh, Kerry.

KERRY: I heard you.

DEL: Look, what is all this?

KERRY: What's all what?

DEL: Well, you've been talking to each other behind my back, I can see that.

BEV: Oh Mum, we're sisters, of course we can talk to each other. And Kerry, don't look at me like that. I . . .

KERRY: Did you tell Mum?

BEV: Oh, for God's sake.

DEL: Well, if you're going to shout about it, then there's no point in discussing it at all.

KERRY: I'm not shouting. Did you tell Mum about what we were talking about?

DEL: I'm going to put you on . . . you're not going out ever again if it's going to be like this.

KERRY: Oh, see what you've done. I told you not to tell her anything about it. She wouldn't understand.

BEV: Oh, come on, Kerry, for God's sake now, just stop shouting and everybody calm down. This is ridiculous.

KERRY: Oh, you sound just like Mum. You shouldn't have told her. I would have brought it up with Mum myself. I didn't want you to tell her.

DEL: So, you have been talking about it.

KERRY: Yes, I have been talking about it.

DEL: Well, why didn't you talk to me about it, then?

KERRY: I was going to.

DEL: Well, talk to me about it now, then.

KERRY: Well, she's obviously said it all, hasn't she?

BEV: No, I haven't . . .

[KEV *enters.*]

KEV: Hey, Del, can I have a cup of tea?

DEL: Look, haven't you got something to do at the bottom of the garden?

[*They all glare at* KEV *who retreats and exits.*]
Now, let's have this out. What's been going on?

BEV: All that's going on is that she's been out with Jeff and she wants to see him again. They're not just playmates, Mum.

KERRY: I'm sixteen. I'm nearly sixteen, Mum.

DEL: Well, that's still very young as far as I'm concerned.

KERRY: It isn't.

BEV: The boy is nearly seventeen, Mum. That's not so young.

DEL: Well, if he wants to go out with somebody and do more than play, he can choose somebody older than my fifteen-year-old daughter, that's all I've got to say about it.

KERRY: Oh, Mum ...

BEV: Kerry ... Mum, he doesn't want somebody else, he wants Kerry. And not just for a screw or a one-night stand.

DEL: Don't use those sorts of words here.

BEV: Don't get hoity-toity about it.

DEL: Well, don't use those sorts of words in my house. I've not had them in here before, and I'm not having them now.

BEV: Mum, that's not what it's all about. They've got something going, and if they do end up in bed, do you want her to get pregnant?

DEL: No. Of course I don't. I think she should just say no.

KERRY: I have. Of course I've said no. I've said no all along.

BEV: Yeah, and I used to say no and look what happened to me.

DEL: I don't want to talk about that, Beverly. There's no need to bring that up again. Besides, you and Brian were going to get married the next year.

KERRY: Hey, what are you two on about?

DEL: It's not important.

BEV: It is important. I don't see why Kerry has to take the same risks as I had to and end up getting pregnant.

DEL: Bev!

BEV: For God's sake. Face it. Why can't she go on the pill?

DEL: No! She can't. I mean, it's all right for you to talk but Kerry is only fifteen. I can't go to Dr Stevens and ask for my fifteen-year-old daughter to be on the pill. I mean, what does it make us look like?

BEV: Well, is that all you're worried about?

DEL: Well, it is a very important thing. I mean, Dr Stevens, I see her in the street, I see her at the bowling. What's she going to think about our family if, if my child . . . she's just a child.

BEV: Mum, she doesn't have to go to Dr Stevens. If Kerry decides that she wants to go on the pill, Family Planning Clinics. Ever heard of those! I can go with her, she can go on her own. Dr Stevens doesn't have to know anything about it.

KERRY: I'm not saying I want to go on it either, Mum. She said that I had to talk to you about it, that's all. I'm not saying that I'm gonna do it. I just want to know what to do.

BEV: I didn't want her doing it behind your back. It had to be brought out into the open.

DEL: Oh, look, I can't say yes . . . I just can't say yes. I know, I . . . It's very disappointing. It's very . . . I know things have changed, but I can't help feeling that she's so young, Bev.

BEV: I know she's young, but how disappointed would you be if she was pregnant?

DEL: Oh, look, I just can't talk about it. I can't take her, and I don't want you to take her either. Not yet. Think about it, just for a little bit, please.

BEV: I'm only thinking about what's best for her.

DEL: I know you are, but she's just a child.

BEV: I know she's just a child, but if she's going to sleep with someone, then . . .

DEL: Then she shouldn't. I don't think she should.

KERRY: Oh, you just don't understand.

[BEV *and* DEL *exit*.]

SCENE TEN

KERRY *goes to the telephone.* JEFF *enters. They ring each other at the same time. They hang up.* KERRY *rings again.* JEFF *answers.*

JEFF: Hello?

KERRY: Jeff?
JEFF: Hi.
KERRY: Gee, that was quick.
JEFF: Yeah, I was ringing you.
KERRY: Were ya? I was ringing you.
JEFF: Oh yeah . . . Ah, listen, Kerry —
KERRY: I wanna talk to ya.
JEFF: Yeah, I wanted to talk to you.
KERRY: But not on the phone.
JEFF: Oh, yeah, OK. Can I come to your place?
KERRY: Yeah, that'd be good. What about now?
JEFF: Right, see ya.
KERRY: Bye.

THE END

Wasting Away

David Young

Susan Kennedy as Rosie in the Toe Truck Theatre production of *Wasting Away*. Photo by Sandy Edwards.

FOREWORD

This is not a play about a trendy but nonetheless comparatively rare disease that affects teenage girls, it is a play about certain regrettable conditions of our society that affect everyone, female and male, young and old. Most of us, willingly or otherwise, endure these conditions, and as a result sell short our potential as human beings. In our efforts to play the roles, particularly the sex-roles, seemingly demanded of us, we limit our possibilities both as individuals and as members of communities — in short, we waste ourselves.

We do this all our lives, but it is as teenagers that we are particularly vulnerable to the pressures that make us do it. As we teeter on the brink of adulthood, we are subjected to a greater bombardment of these pressures — frequently in complete and confusing contradiction to one another — than at any other time; our friends, our parents, our idols, our teachers and — dominating and determining the attitudes of all these — those willing tools of rapacious capital, the media, hound and cajole us daily; and most of us finally succumb. Whatever our initial resistance, we eventually make the decision to tell — and to believe — just enough lies to achieve social acceptability.

But fortunately some young people don't. Some have the courage to reject the sham values that are foisted on them from all sides, to give two fingers to social acceptability, and they rebel. Anorexia nervosa is one form of rebellion, of simply saying 'no', and of saying it in several profound and uncompromising ways:

- In the first place, it says no to control: 'No, you cannot make me eat, I alone control that, therefore I am my own person.'

- In the second place, it says no to normality: 'No, I do not eat as you do, I do not do as you do, I choose to be different, I *dare* to be different, therefore I am different.'

- In the third place, it says no to adulthood: 'No, my body will not mature as yours will, for by not feeding it I will not let it go through the changes that yours will go through; I will stop both it and myself from having to cope with the awfulness of being grown up.'

- And in the final place, in extremis, it says no to life itself: it kills.

Wasting Away is not intended to put the case for anorexia nervosa; on the contrary, it is intended to attack the values of a society which breeds and fosters such a wasteful perversity, and to incite the young people who see the play into wanting to change *that* rather than themselves.

David Young, May, 1984

DAVID YOUNG was Artistic Director of Toe Truck Theatre during 1984. He entered theatre-in-education in 1972 when he joined the Coventry (UK) TIE team as an actor/teacher, later becoming the company's writer/researcher. During the mid-seventies, he was artistic director of Arena Theatre, Melbourne. As a freelance director and writer, he has worked with companies in South Australia (Magpie), Western Australia (NTC) and Tasmania (Salamanca). His plays, which have been performed in all Australian states and territories with the exception of Queensland include *Num Lagger (White Man Come)*, *Eureka*, *The Price of Coal*, and *Wasting Away*. His most recent production for Toe Truck Theatre was Bob Maza's *Mereki (The Peace-maker)*. He has recently taken up the position of Artistic Director of Salamanca Theatre, Tasmania.

Wasting Away was first performed by the Theatre-in-Education team of the National Theatre Company, Perth, at South Fremantle Senior High School on 15 June 1982 with the following cast:

ROSIE
ACTOR 1

Timm Goddard

SALESGIRL
MRS SYMONDS
TRISH
ACTOR 2

Di Shaw

TERRY
MR SYMONDS
ACTOR 3

Brian Peddie

PETER
MR BUTLER
DOCTOR
ACTOR 4

John Butler

MANDY
PSYCHIATRIST
ACTOR 5

Shirley van Sanden

Directed by John Preston
Designed by Jenny Muir

The revised version which follows was first performed by Toe Truck Theatre, Sydney, at Wawina Creative Secondary School, Balmain, on 21 February 1984 with the following cast:

ROSIE   Susan Kennedy
ACTOR 1

SALESGIRL   Mercia Deane-Johns
MRS SYMONDS
TRISH
ACTOR 2

MANAGER   Barry Langrish
TERRY
MR SYMONDS
ACTOR 3

PETER   Ian Pidd
MR BUTLER
DOCTOR
ACTOR 4

MANDY   Peta Rutter
PSYCHIATRIST
ACTOR 5

Directed by David Young
Designed by Trina Parker

AUTHOR'S NOTE

The author would like to thank both companies and particularly his wife, Sandi Greentree, for the many suggestions and words of advice that helped to develop the final version of the script.

CHARACTERS

> ROSIE, a repressed and confused sixteen-year-old
> MRS SYMONDS, Rosie's mother
> TRISH, a student at Rosie's school
> MR SYMONDS, Rosie's father
> TERRY, a student at Rosie's school
> PETER, Rosie's younger brother
> MR BUTLER, a teacher
> DOCTOR
> MANDY, Rosie's school friend
> PSYCHIATRIST
> BOUTIQUE MANAGER
> SALESGIRL

SETTING

The play takes place in Rosie's home and school, in a boutique and in the psychiatric ward of a hospital.

WASTING AWAY

SCENE ONE

ACTOR 1 *enters, dressed in school uniform.*

ACTOR 1: [*to the audience*] Hi, my name's . . . and I'm from the . . . Company. The play we're presenting today is called *Wasting Away*. It's about a girl who develops a condition known as anorexia nervosa, sometimes known as 'the slimmers disease'.

> [*Immediately, we hear 'The Peter Gun Theme', preferably the version by The Blues Brothers. From each side of the set emerge* ACTORS 3 *and* 4, *dressed in tight jeans and dark glasses, they strut towards* ACTOR 1 *until they flank her. She shrinks away from them nervously, having adopted the character of* ROSIE, *a repressed and confused sixteen-year-old. Simultaneously, the men clap their hands. From each side emerge* ACTORS 2 *and* 5. *Dressed in alarmingly tight jeans and dark glasses, they bump and grind towards the audience. Simultaneously, they stop.*]

ACTORS 3 and 4: [*pointing to the women*] Thigh-clinging!

> [*The women pose to demonstrate this attribute of their jeans. The men look at* ROSIE *to make sure she has taken the point. This sequence is repeated after each adjective that follows.*]

Hip-hugging! Bottom-pinching!
Groin-grabbing! Man-trapping!

> [*The music stops and the men turn to* ROSIE.]

But only wear them if you dare!

> [*As the music reaches a climax, the women adopt a series of pseudo-erotic poses. The music stops and 'Fashion' by David Bowie is faded in. It continues at a low level under the rest of the scene.* ACTOR 4 *exits and the others take up positions ready for the scene proper,*

which is set in a boutique. The SALESGIRL *and the
(Italian)* MANAGER *arrange clothes on a rack.* ROSIE
waits outside a cubicle.]

ROSIE: Come on, Mandy.

MANDY: [*inside the cubicle*]
  Hey, why don't you try some on?

ROSIE: No, Mandy.

MANDY: [*inside cubicle*] Just try one pair.

ROSIE: I told you, I haven't got time.

MANDY: [*Emerging from the cubicle wearing a pair of
  bright, skin-tight jeans*] Yeah, I know. You're supposed to
  be home. God, you can be a drag, Rosie. De-dah! ...
  Well, what d'ya reckon?

ROSIE: [*shrugging*] OK.

MANDY: Just OK?

ROSIE: Well, they'd only be about the millionth pair you've
  tried on.

MANDY: So? ... You gotta take a bit of trouble, you know.

ROSIE: Trouble!

SALEGIRL: [*taking a belt over to* MANDY] Wow! They're fantastic, eh?

ROSIE: Bit tight, I reckon.

SALESGIRL: Tight?

MANDY: Tight is the rage, Rosie.

ROSIE: Might as well paint your legs as have them that tight.
  Be a lot cheaper.

SALESGIRL: [*to* MANDY] Gawd!

MANDY: It's OK. She's just scared to wear them. 'Case they
  make her look too spunky. Eh, Rosie?

ROSIE: Bull!

MANDY: OK then. Next Sat'dee. End of term rage. Turn up
  in some. I dare you!

ROSIE: Mandee!

MANDY: Or are *you* chicken?

ROSIE: 'Course not.

SALESGIRL: [*quickly*] Right, see what I can find.
    [*She goes out, followed by the* MANAGER.]

ROSIE: What! Jeez, Mandy! I haven't even said for sure I'm
  going to the end of term rage.

MANDY: Course you are.
ROSIE: Why?
MANDY: 'Cos everyone does.
ROSIE: So?
MANDY: Ah, come on, Rosie.
ROSIE: What d'ya mean: come on?
MANDY: You don't go to dances, you don't go on dates . . .
ROSIE: Anything else?
MANDY: Yeah. You look like a dag, and you don't even care!
ROSIE: Thanks.
MANDY: Well, it's true.

[ROSIE *turns her back. The* SALESGIRL *returns carrying a pair of jeans. The* MANAGER *follows her.*]

SALESGIRL: These should fit.
ROSIE: No thanks.
SALESGIRL: Try them.
ROSIE: Haven't got time.
SALESGIRL: Won't take a minute.
MANDY: Go on, Rosie.

[*The* SALESGIRL *holds up the jeans for inspection.*]

ROSIE: They wouldn't suit me.
MANDY: Sure they would.
MANAGER: They'd make you look fantastic . . . just like your friend.
SALESGIRL: (*moving to the cubicle*) Go on. You don't have to buy them . . .
ROSIE: God, I don't know. I reckon I must be mad!

[*She takes the jeans and goes into the cubicle.*]

SALESGIRL: . . . and if you like them . . .
ROSIE: [*inside cubicle*] Which I won't.
SALESGIRL: [*unperturbed*] . . . I can always hold them a coupla days.
ROSIE: [*inside cubicle*] Thanks. But even if I did like them, I couldn't afford them.
MANDY: So get your Mum to pay.
ROSIE: Ha, ha! [*Emerging from the cubicle wearing the jeans, which are tight, but do not flatter her figure*] Well?
MANDY: [*about to deliver an honest opinion*] Well —
MANAGER: [*looking at* MANDY] Fantastic, eh?

MANDY: Fantastic.

> [*They all look at* ROSIE. *She regards herself. 'Snack Attack' by Godley and Creme is heard.*]

SCENE TWO

The Symonds' dining room. ROSIE *and* PETER, *her younger brother, are seated at the table, frozen in the position of finishing their tea.* ACTOR 2 *enters, dressed as* MRS SYMONDS. *The character she adopts for the time being is that of 'The Cosy Mum' of the television commercials.*

ACTOR 2: [*to the audience*] Maybe I'm old-fashioned, but it's my belief that the evening meal is the most important aspect of the family's day. And, as an old-fashioned Mum, I like to get it right. With Gravox! [*Holding up a packet*] Still making gravy the way my mother made it. Gravox, the gravy maker for families that care about being families.

> [PETER *and* ROSIE *animate.* ACTOR 2 *becomes* MRS SYMONDS.]

PETER: [*getting up*] Gotta go, Mum.

MRS SYMONDS: Not till you've finished.

PETER: Ah, Mum!

MRS SYMONDS: Peter!

> [PETER *resumes his seat, and begins to stuff all the food on his plate into his mouth very rapidly.*]

PETER: Be great if I miss the bus. Terrific!

MRS SYMONDS: If you do, the others will simply have to start without you.

PETER: Wasn't my fault dinner was late —

MRS SYMONDS: And don't talk with your mouth full!

PETER: [*after a few moments of angry eating*] OK? Can I go now?

MRS SYMONDS: When you've finished chewing.

> [PETER *chews energetically and angrily. He swallows and then shows his empty mouth.*]

PETER: Satisfied?

[MRS SYMONDS *nods tightly.* PETER *gets up and grabs a violin case lying near the table. He goes.*]

Thanks, Rosie!

MRS SYMONDS: [*calling after him*] And be sure you're back by ten!

ROSIE: Fat chance.

MRS SYMONDS: If he isn't, his father'll have something to say.

ROSIE: [*muttering*] *When* he gets home.

MRS SYMONDS: [*sharply*] He'll get home when he finishes work... Anyway, you're a fine one to talk about lateness.

ROSIE: [*cowed*] I've said I'm sorry.

MRS SYMONDS: You know I rely on you to help get tea ready, Rosie.

ROSIE: Yes, Mum.

MRS SYMONDS: Well then?

ROSIE: Well...

MRS SYMONDS: Yes?

ROSIE: Well, why me all the time? Why not Peter?

MRS SYMONDS: He washes the car, mows the lawn —

ROSIE: Once in a blue moon!

MRS SYMONDS: Anyway, you know what men are like around the house. Completely useless!

ROSIE: [*helping her mother clear the table*] That's right, there are some jobs that women just naturally do best.

MRS SYMONDS: Well, there are.

ROSIE: If you ask me, men get it pretty easy.

MRS SYMONDS: They've got their responsibilities too.

ROSIE: What reponsibilities has Peter got?

MRS SYMONDS: Peter's only fifteen.

ROSIE: Well, I'm only sixteen, but I can't go out like he does. Playing music every night.

MRS SYMONDS: [*folding the tablecloth*] It's not just pop music, Rosie. It is the school orchestra, as you well know. And moreover Peter's potentially a very talented musician. Mr Butler said so. So it would be hardly fair for your father and I to stand in his way, now would it? Honestly?

ROSIE: No, but...

MRS SYMONDS: Well?

ROSIE: [*weakly*] Well. . .

MRS SYMONDS: You've really got to stop this silly jealousy of your brother, Rosie.

 [*She takes the cloth into the kitchen.*]

ROSIE: [*yelling after her*] I'm not jealous! It's just that sometimes I might like to go out too, and not be cooped up here all the time, helping round the house and doing rotten homework.

MRS SYMONDS: [*emerging with a glass*] Well, this is news to me.

ROSIE: Is it?

MRS SYMONDS: You've never mentioned it before. I've always assumed you were sensible enough to realise that homework comes first. Until you get accepted by uni, anyway. Then you can relax a little.

 [*She sits and sips.*]

ROSIE: It's all plotted out for me, isn't it?

MRS SYMONDS: What is?

ROSIE: Life.

MRS SYMONDS: Now, don't be silly —

ROSIE: I'm not. You and Dad have decided that every night I should do my homework like a sensible girl, then you've decided I'm going to uni, becoming a doctor —

MRS SYMONDS: And what's wrong with becoming a doctor?

ROSIE: Nothing. . . I'm just not sure if that's what I want to do.

MRS SYMONDS: Well, what do you want to do? Potter round boutiques all day with silly Mandy, spending money willy-nilly: what kind of mindless existence is that?

ROSIE: I don't see what's mindless about wanting new clothes once in a while. Everyone else at school's got nice gear. What have I got? Nothing! Zero!

MRS SYMONDS: Well, I don't think —

ROSIE: Anyway, I've put a pair of jeans on lay-by.

MRS SYMONDS: You've what?

ROSIE: Put a pair of jeans on lay-by. . . this afternoon.

 [*Pause.*]

MRS SYMONDS: How much?

ROSIE: Thirty-two ninety-five.

MRS SYMONDS: Rosie!

ROSIE: I've got the money.

MRS SYMONDS: In your savings maybe, but that's —

ROSIE: For when I'm at uni, I know. Till then, what am I? I'll tell you: I'm Rosie the dag!

    [Pause.]

MRS SYMONDS: Well, what's brought all this on suddenly?

ROSIE: *[abruptly]* There's a senior school dance on Saturday night: I've decided to go.

MRS SYMONDS: I see.

ROSIE: Everyone else'll be going.

    [Pause.]

MRS SYMONDS: I'm not stopping you from going, Rosie. *[Getting up]* I'm just a bit surprised, that's all. I mean, you're not usually interested.

    [She walks towards the kitchen.]

ROSIE: And the jeans?

MRS SYMONDS: *[turning at the door]* We'll see what your father says.

ROSIE: Mum!

MRS SYMONDS: Well, they are thirty-three dollars, Rosie. Suppose you only wore them once.

ROSIE: I wouldn't!

MRS SYMONDS: You say that now —

ROSIE: I knew it!

    [Pause.]

MRS SYMONDS: Look, I'll tell you what. How about if we go to the shop together; then we'll decide, eh?

ROSIE: You mean it, Mum?

MRS SYMONDS: Of course I do, love. Of course I mean it.

    ['Beat it' by Michael Jackson is heard.]

SCENE THREE

The school hall. It is the night of the dance, and the music continues under the scene. MANDY *is on stage in her tight jeans.* ROSIE *enters wearing a dress obviously chosen for her by her mother. She approaches* MANDY.

ROSIE: [*tentatively*] Hi, Mandy.

MANDY: Christ, Rosie, what're you wearing?

ROSIE: Don't you like it?

MANDY: Where are the jeans?

ROSIE: Oh, I changed my mind. Thirty-three bucks, Mandy!

MANDY: Didn't worry you Wednesday.

ROSIE: Yeah, well . . .

MANDY: You should've bought them, Rosie. They looked good on you. Whereas that . . . What'd it cost anyhow?

ROSIE: I dunno . . . Somewhere round —

MANDY: You don't know? . . . You did choose it yourself, didn't you?

ROSIE: Course I did.

MANDY: [*sceptically*] Hmmm.

ROSIE: I told you: I thought the jeans were too tight.

MANDY: But you changed your mind when you tried them on.

ROSIE: I changed it back again then, didn't I?

MANDY: Yeah . . . or your mum did.

ROSIE: I did! I don't want to spend thirty-three dollars on something I might only wear once.

MANDY: Sounds like your mum talking to me.

ROSIE: [*now furious*] And I didn't want to turn up looking like a moll either.

MANDY: A moll?

ROSIE: That's what I said.

MANDY: A moll! Is that what you reckon I look like?

ROSIE: If the cap fits . . .

MANDY: A moll! Well, if I look like a moll, what the hell d'you reckon you look like, eh Rosie? What do you look like?

    [*'Beat it' cross-fades into Mozart's Piano Concerto No. 21.* ACTOR 2, *still dressed as* MRS SYMONDS, *enters. As she speaks to the audience, she takes* ROSIE *by the hand, and parades her round.*]

ACTOR 2: The Girl-Next-Door look is today's in fashion for

those discerning mothers who want to keep their daughters looking like daughters. With softly hanging sleeves, full skirts and delicate lacework, it's so delightfully and decoratively different. Designed for girls who don't have to pretend to be anything but girls.

> [ACTOR 2 *exits. The piano concerto cross-fades back into 'Beat it'.*]

MANDY: Well?

> [TERRY *enters.*]

There's Terry. I'll ask him, will I?

ROSIE: Don't expect me to hang around if you do.

MANDY: Too bad.

ROSIE: Well . . . see ya then!

> [MANDY *moves slinkily over towards* TERRY, *while* ROSIE *looks on, horrified.*]

MANDY: Hi, Terry.

TERRY: [*preoccupied with eyeing up girls*] Oh, hi.

MANDY: Like my new jeans?

TERRY: Eh? Yeah, they're OK.

MANDY: Rosie reckons they make me look like a moll.

TERRY: A moll?

MANDY: [*running her hands seductively over her jeans*] That's what she said, Terry.

TERRY: [*succumbing to* MANDY*'s charms*] Well, what'd she know, eh?

MANDY: [*yelling*] Hear that, Rosie?

TERRY: [*encouraged*] Anyhow, what does she reckon she looks like, eh, Mand?

MANDY: That's what I asked her.

TERRY: That right?

MANDY: Yep.

TERRY: Well, she sure is a dag.

MANDY: She sure is.

> [*They both begin to dance.* ROSIE *hesitates a moment, and then leaves.* MANDY *notices that she has gone, and stops dancing.*]

TERRY: What's up?

MANDY: She's gone.

TERRY: So?

[*Slight pause.*]

MANDY: Nothing, I guess.

[*They dance on,* MANDY *looking a shade uneasy. The music stops.*]

SCENE FOUR

Rosie's room. ROSIE *enters, still wearing her dress. She is upset, and throws herself into a chair.* MRS SYMONDS *follows her into the room.*

MRS SYMONDS: Well, I don't see how it can all have been my fault.

ROSIE: If you'd let me wear the jeans —

MRS SYMONDS: But you agreed with me. You agreed they were too tight.

ROSIE: Did I have a choice?

[*Pause.*]

MRS SYMONDS: All right, I'll admit I obviously chose something inappropriate for one of your dances. But suppose I had let you have the jeans. What would probably have happened? You would have come home, tried them on, taken a look in the mirror where there's enough light to see properly, and away from all that silly music in the clothes shop, and you would have understood why they were wrong for you.

ROSIE: Why?

[*Pause.*]

Why?

MRS SYMONDS: Well, if you must know, Rosie, they made you look, well . . . fat, dear.

ROSIE: Fat?

MRS SYMONDS: Plump, anyway.

ROSIE: I'm not fat . . . or plump!

[*She gets up and looks in the mirror.*]

MRS SYMONDS: Have it your own way . . . But why should I say you were, if you weren't?

ROSIE: Where? . . . Where am I fat?
MRS SYMONDS: Don't get upset, Rosie.
ROSIE: [*still looking*] Where?
MRS SYMONDS: It's just puppy-fat; it'll go away.
ROSIE: Puppy-fat?
MRS SYMONDS: Most teenage girls get it. I had it when I was
    your age.
ROSIE: [*ironically*] That's comforting to know.
MRS SYMONDS: [*reacting angrily*] Look, Rosie, I've told you
    before, there's plenty of time to worry about looks and at-
    tracting boys. You're only sixteen —
ROSIE: So are most of the girls in my class —
MRS SYMONDS: Yes, and heaven knows what most of them
    get up to.
ROSIE: What do you mean?
MRS SYMONDS: You know very well. You only have to read
    the papers . . . [*breaking off in distaste*] No, you're better
    off getting on with your studies. Let other girls waste their
    time on boutiques and discos and boyfriends.
ROSIE: Just as well I'm fat and ugly then, isn't it?
MRS SYMONDS: You're not ugly, Rosie. 'Specially if you take
    my advice and dress sensibly. There's nothing wrong with
    your figure that can't be hidden by the right clothes.
ROSIE: [*ironically*] Thanks, Mum.
MRS SYMONDS: Well, there's nothing else you can do. You're
    just going through a stage that you've got to accept for a
    couple of years. And that's all there is to it.
    [*Pause.*]
I'm sorry your evening was spoiled, Rosie. But, if it's any
consolation, I think you look very pretty in that dress.
And so does your father.
ROSIE: [*with a flicker of a smile*] Thanks, Mum.
MRS SYMONDS: I'll just go and put the kettle on.
    [*She leaves.* ROSIE *goes back to the mirror, and exam-
    ines herself critically from several angles.*]
ROSIE: Yuck!
    [*Chord on a harp.* ACTOR 5, *dressed as a fairy, enters.*]
ACTOR 5: [*to audience*] Yes, if that's what you think when
    you look in the mirror, then what you need is Ford Slim-

ming Tabs.

[*She uses her wand on* ROSIE*'s body to demonstrate her points to the audience.* ROSIE *uses whatever means she can to conceal each named 'unsatisfactory' part of her body.*]

You need Weight-Watchers [*touching* ROSIE*'s backside*], Limmits [*stomach*], Lo-Cal [*thigh*], Trimmers [*other thigh*], vibrators [*hip*], saunas [*other hip*] and silicone inserts [*bust*]. To tone up that flabby flesh, may I recommend Helancyl Massage Regime (used by over a million Frenchwomen), Ego Skin Cream and Veto for that unwanted body hair [*armpits*], Free 'n' Lovely [*hair*], Dr Scholl [*feet*] and Yardley's Oatmeal Foam [*face*]. And, of course, for that more personal region, may I recommend Femfresh [*crutch*] ... Yes, girls, for just a little extra effort and a little extra expense, that ideal eye-catching face and figure can be yours!

[*Chord on a harp.* ACTOR 5 *leaves.* ROSIE*'s body is utterly contorted. 'House of Fun' by Madness is heard.*]

SCENE FIVE

The Symonds' dining room. MRS SYMONDS, ROSIE *and* PETER *sit at the table.* ACTOR 3 *stands and addresses the audience, piously, in the role of patriarch.*

ACTOR 3: Sunday lunch. More than a meal — an institution! Baked potatoes, roast beef: delicious!

[*He taps the table. The family sit bolt upright.* ACTOR 3 *conducts the family in three-part harmony.*]

FAMILY: Feed the man

Feed the man

Feed the man — MEAT!

[ACTOR 3 *sits, and becomes* MR SYMONDS. *They begin eating. Soon* ROSIE *puts down her knife and fork.*]

MRS SYMONDS: You haven't finished, Rosie, surely?

ROSIE: Sorry, Mum. I'm bloated.

MRS SYMONDS: But your potatoes. You haven't touched
  them.
ROSIE: I told you I didn't want any.
MRS SYMONDS: But they're baked potatoes, Rosie. Your
  favourites.
ROSIE: I still told you, Mum... Sorry.
PETER: [*seizing his moment*] I'll have them.
  [*He reaches for* ROSIE's *plate.*]
MRS SYMONDS: Peter!
PETER: Eh?
MR SYMONDS: [*taking charge*] Look, in this house no
  shovelling food off one plate and onto another. Right!
PETER: OK, so chuck it out. Who cares?
MR SYMONDS: Nor will it be 'chucked out'. Will it, Rosie?
  [ROSIE *doesn't answer.*]
  Because your mother and I have just about had a bellyful
  of this food fad nonsense —
ROSIE: To coin a phrase.
MR SYMONDS: Well, you can be smart if you like, but it
  won't change the facts. We've had enough of it.
MRS SYMONDS: That's right, Rosie. We've put up with it for
  three weeks now —
ROSIE: Well, if you want a fatso for a daughter...
MRS SYMONDS: I've told you, dear, you won't be plump for
  long.
ROSIE: Too right!
MRS SYMONDS: Look, you've got to have proper nourish-
  ment, or you'll just get sick. Won't she, George?
MR SYMONDS: Of course she will!
ROSIE: But I feel fine, Dad. Really.
MR SYMONDS: Sure! You do now, after your holidays. But
  what about when you're back at school? You'll be keeling
  over in class. And that's not on, Rosie! So, eat your lunch
  up, please! OK?
PETER: Lovely greasy baked potatoes, yum yum.
MR SYMONDS: Shut up, Peter!
PETER: Only trying to help.
MRS SYMONDS: Well, you're not.
  [*Pause. They all look at* ROSIE, *who cuts a piece of*

potato, lifts it on her fork and looks at it. Pause.]
ROSIE: I'm sorry, Mum, I can't.
MR SYMONDS: What does she mean, she can't?
ROSIE: I can't eat it.
MRS SYMONDS: Of course you can.
ROSIE: I can't!
MR SYMONDS: [*exploding*] Well, you're damn well going to! I'm blowed if I'm going to let any more good food go to waste in this house.
MRS SYMONDS: Now, George.
MR SYMONDS: All right, I'm angry! Wasted food makes me angry, very angry! That's because I'm the one who pays for it.
MRS SYMONDS: Well, I'm the one who cooks it.
PETER: And I said I'd eat it.
MR SYMONDS: Peter — shut up!
PETER: God.
    [*Pause.*]
MR SYMONDS: Now, Rosie, listen to me. Your mother's spent hours cooking this food for you, and if all you can do is throw it back in her face —
ROSIE: [*raising her voice*] But I said I didn't want any potatoes. I told Mum! Why didn't she take any notice of me?
    [*Pause.*]
MR SYMONDS: [*calmly and authoritatively*] Because she knows better than you what's good for you. Now, I don't want another word, understand! Just eat!
    [ROSIE *stares at her plate. All look at her. Long pause.*]
PETER: [*singing*] 'Always look on the bright side of — '
    [MR SYMONDS *raps the table hard with his knife.* PETER *shuts up. One by one, the family go back to eating, with the exception of* ROSIE. *She watches the others, her expression indicating her distaste. Eventually,* PETER *looks up.*]
May I be excused, please, Father?
MR SYMONDS: [*gruffly*] Yes, go on.
PETER: [*ultra politely*] So kind.
    [*He goes.*]

ROSIE: May I?

MR SYMONDS: No.

MRS SYMONDS: [*simultaneously*] I think —

[*Pause.* MR SYMONDS *looks inquiringly at his wife.*]
She might as well, George.

MR SYMONDS: What?

MRS SYMONDS: She might as well. . . don't you think?

[*Pause.*]

ROSIE: Thanks, Mum. [*Indicating her plate*] Sorry. . .

[*She goes.* MR SYMONDS *waits for her to clear the stage completely before speaking. Meanwhile,* MRS SYMONDS *has started to clear the table.*]

MR SYMONDS: All right, why?

MRS SYMONDS: Well, I'm sorry, George, but —

MR SYMONDS: You know we agreed —

MRS SYMONDS: Yes, I know, but —

MR SYMONDS: So why did you contradict me in front of Rosie?

MRS SYMONDS: Well, it occurred to me, George —

MR SYMONDS: [*impatiently*] Yes?

MRS SYMONDS: . . . that probably it's just a phase she's going through —

MR SYMONDS: Phase!

MRS SYMONDS: . . . and the less we draw attention to it, the quicker it will probably pass.

MR SYMONDS: Really? . . . You think so?

MRS SYMONDS: Yes . . . I think so.

MR SYMONDS: So what do you intend to do: just let her get away with it?

MRS SYMONDS: Just let me handle it my way, eh?

MR SYMONDS: As long as you know what you're doing, I will.

MRS SYMONDS: Look, give me some credit, George. Please! I let you look after the money side of things —

MR SYMONDS: You what? You *let me* look after it?

MRS SYMONDS: Well, whatever. You *do* look after it. I don't interfere, that's your job. Mine's looking after the household, which includes the kids. So please let me do it. Without interfering with *me!* All right?

[*Pause.*]

MR SYMONDS: If that's what you want, it's all yours.
   [*He gets up to leave, but turns at the door.*]
  And *if* Rosie gets sick, you can deal with it yourself. Is *that*
  'all right'?
   [*He goes.*]
MRS SYMONDS: I think I'll manage, thank you.
   [*'Ballad of Lucy Jordan' by Marianne Faithful is
   heard.*]

SCENE SIX

Rosie's room. ROSIE *is trying on a pair of blue denim jeans.
They look a little baggy on her, and certainly not sexy. She
zips them, feels the legs and back with her hands and poses
in front of the mirror.* MRS SYMONDS *enters, carrying a cup
of cocoa and a plate of biscuits. She watches* ROSIE, *who catches sight of her and spins round guiltily.*

MRS SYMONDS: Supper.
   [*She puts down the plate and looks at the jeans.*]
  They're very nice, Rosie. A good fit.
ROSIE: Only cost fifteen dollars.
MRS SYMONDS: [*holding up her hand to silence her*] Uh! It's
  your money, and I trust you to spend it sensibly. Turn
  around.
   [ROSIE *does so.*]
ROSIE: We're allowed to wear them to school now, instead of
  skirts.
MRS SYMONDS: Seems very sensible.
ROSIE: Much warmer.
   [*Pause.*]
MRS SYMONDS: So I was wrong.
ROSIE: Mum?
MRS SYMONDS: About the puppy-fat. You did get rid of it.
ROSIE: [*uncertainly*] Well...
   [*She looks critically in the mirror at herself.*]
MRS SYMONDS: You wouldn't want to be much slimmer,

would you?

ROSIE: S'pose not.

   [*Pause.*]

MRS SYMONDS: [*sitting*] So you're growing up at last, Rosie.
   I can remember myself at your age: slimming, fashion,
   make-up ... Perhaps I've tried to hold you back, keep
   you a little girl too long, but ... oh, I don't know, I just
   sometimes think it's silly to want to grow up too fast.
   Men'll rule your life soon enough, Rosie. So why rush it?

   [ROSIE *pulls a wry face. Uncomfortable pause.* MRS
   SYMONDS *gets up and moves towards the door.*]

   Well, I'd better let you get on with your homework, Rosie.
   Dad'll be glad you've stopped slimming.

ROSIE: [*hurriedly*] But I didn't say —

MRS SYMONDS: You have stopped, haven't you, Rosie?

ROSIE: Well, I'm certainly not going to get fat again.

MRS SYMONDS: No, of course not, but ... well, you've got to
   eat sensibly.

ROSIE: [*priggishly*] I think I know how much food my body
   needs.

MRS SYMONDS: Well, maybe.

ROSIE: It is *my* body, after all.

MRS SYMONDS: I know, dear —

ROSIE: So why not let *me* decide what's best for it?

   [*Pause.*]

MRS SYMONDS: Yes, of course, dear ... But, well, I can tell
   your father that you've ... that you're not trying to lose
   any more weight, at least? Can't I?

ROSIE: I don't see what it's got to do with him.

MRS SYMONDS: Rosie!

   [*Pause.*]

   Well, can I or can't I?

   [*Pause.*]

ROSIE: Sure. I'm thin enough.

MRS SYMONDS: [*with relief*] Good ... Well, I'll leave you to
   it. Don't let your cocoa get cold.

   [*She goes.* ROSIE *waits. Then she picks up her cup and
   plate and goes to the door. She looks around and then
   goes out. Three seconds pass. A toilet flushes.* ROSIE *re-*

enters. She puts the plate down, and the cup upside down on top of it. Her expression is at once smug and sly. She goes back to the mirror, and continues to examine herself. 'I Know What Boys Want' by The Waitresses is heard.]

SCENE SEVEN

A school yard. ACTORS 3 *and* 4 *carry out the set change dressed in jeans and singlets. Their manner is aggressively macho. When they have finished, they fall into a pose such as might be found in a fashion magazine, only more so.* ACTORS 5 *and* 2 *enter. They are dressed as schoolgirls, but their manner initially is more sophisticated than one would expect. They pose for the audience on either side of the men.* ACTOR 5 *carries a copy of* Cleo.

ACTOR 5: *Cleo* — the magazine for today's liberated lady.
ACTOR 2: How she can trap her man ...
    [ACTORS 3 *and* 4 *strike a new pose after this and each of the succeeding phrases.*]
ACTOR 5: Please her boss ...
ACTOR 2: Please her lover ...
ACTOR 5: Please her family ...
ACTOR 2: Please herself ...
ACTOR 5: And achieve success as a woman in today's ...
ACTORS 2 *and* 5: ... man's world.
    [ACTORS 3 *and* 4 *leave.* ACTORS 5 *and* 2 *become* MANDY *and* TRISH *respectively.* MANDY *opens the magazine at the centrefold and gawks.*]
TRISH: Come on, give us a look.
MANDY: Hang on!
    [TRISH *grabs the magazine and looks for herself.*]
TRISH: Ooh, isn't he sexy.
MANDY: Give it back! You'll tear it! Trish!
TRISH: OK, we'll both look.
    [*They do so, pointing out details.* ROSIE *enters, carry-*

ing a lunchbox. She passes MANDY *and* TRISH *without acknowledgement, and sits down.* TRISH *sees her, and watches while she opens her lunchbox, takes something out and nibbles at it.* TRISH *nudges* MANDY.]

Hey. What's she eating?

MANDY: Celery.

[ROSIE *nibbles a bit more.*]

TRISH: D'you reckon it's a sex substitute?

[TRISH *and* MANDY *snort with suppressed mirth.* ROSIE *looks around suspiciously.*]

MANDY: Sssh! She'll hear us.

TRISH: So what?

MANDY: Well . . .

TRISH: Still your mate, is she?

MANDY: Yeah . . . s'pose so.

TRISH: So what's she doing sitting by herself

MANDY: Dunno. Maybe she just wants to be alone.

TRISH: She's hardly talked to anyone all term.

[MANDY *shrugs.*]

Wonder what she's thinking.

[*Suddenly* TRISH *makes an impulsive grab for the* Cleo, *takes it and goes over to* ROSIE.]

MANDY: [*trying in vain to restrain her*] Trish!

TRISH: Hi, Rosie. [*Displaying the centrefold*] This what's on your mind?

[MANDY *saunters over somewhat sheepishly behind* TRISH. *She stands on the other side of* ROSIE. ROSIE *looks at the centrefold, then at* TRISH, *then up at* MANDY.]

MANDY: [*coyly*] Hi, Rosie.

TRISH: Sooner nibble that than celery, eh?

ROSIE: God, you're childish, you two.

MANDY: Me? What's it got to do with me?

TRISH: And what's childish about it anyway?

ROSIE: Well, if you don't know...

TRISH: No, I don't. So tell me.

ROSIE: Perving on naked men. It's pretty mindless, isn't it?

TRISH: [*to* MANDY] She'd rather perv on her physics books . . . Bet she's never seen a naked man anyway.

ROSIE: I wouldn't want to.

TRISH: Hear that? She's not normal.

ROSIE: Well, Trish, if you're a typical example of the norm —

TRISH: 'The norm'! Get her! I'm a 'typical example of the norm', Mandy.

ROSIE: [*standing*] 'Scuse me.

MANDY: What's the matter, Rosie?

ROSIE: What d'you think?

TRISH: Oh God, we've driven her away. Gnash gnash, wail wail, sob.

ROSIE: Look, all I want is to have my lunch in peace, OK?

TRISH: Lunch? She calls this lunch, Mandy!

   [*She picks something out of* ROSIE's *box, and holds it up for inspection.*]

ROSIE: Do you mind?

MANDY: Yeah, come on, Trish.

TRISH: [*to* MANDY] Well of all the stuck-up, snobbish —

ROSIE: I'll tell you something, Trish: I'd sooner be a snob than swallow all the bullshit you swallow —

TRISH: What bullshit? . . . Oh, you mean this?

   [*She holds up the* Cleo. ROSIE *does not answer.* TRISH *goes over to her.*]

   I bet you've never even been out with a boy, have you? . . . Yeah, what boy in his right mind would want to go out with you, *Bones*?

MANDY: Trish!

ROSIE: That's all right, Mandy. I really couldn't give a stuff.

MANDY: That was a bit heavy, Trish.

   [TRISH *sneers.* MANDY *walks over to* ROSIE.]

   Rosie.

ROSIE: What?

MANDY: [*at a loss*] You all right?

ROSIE: [*tightly*] Fine, thank you.

   [*Pause.*]

MANDY: That wasn't my idea, you know. Coming over with —

ROSIE: Look, forget it! OK?

MANDY: OK.

[*Awkward pause.* MANDY *turns round and catches* TRISH'S *eye.* TRISH *walks off in a huff.* MANDY *turns back to* ROSIE.]
Rosie.

ROSIE: What?

MANDY: Well ... [*With sudden resolve*] Look, you've been steering clear of me all term, haven't you?

ROSIE: Have I?

MANDY: You know damn well you have! Look, if it's because of that dance —

ROSIE: Dance? What dance?

MANDY: The dance at the end of last term. Christ, Rosie! ... Look, if it's because of that, I'm sorry. I shouldn't have rubbished your dress ... OK?

    [*Pause.*]

ROSIE: [*non-committally*] That's all right, Mandy.

MANDY: Good ... Well, what you doing on the weekend?

ROSIE: The weekend?

MANDY: Yeah, want to come over?

ROSIE: [*surprised*] Oh, I ...

MANDY: Hey, I've got an idea.

ROSIE: What?

MANDY: Well, Sat'dee night I'm going out with Terry, right? Now, he's got a mate, Brian, you don't know him, goes to another school — [*Noticing that* ROSIE'S *face has fallen, and breaking off*] What's the matter?

ROSIE: Well —

MANDY: Come on, Rosie. It'd be fun ... We could go skating, make up a foursome ... And, anyway, it'd be good if you went out with a feller. Just to prove Trish wrong.

ROSIE: [*frosting up*] I really couldn't care about Trish, Mandy.

MANDY: [*proceeding cautiously*] Yeah, but even so ... you don't want her to put it about that you're some kind of freak, do you?

ROSIE: Of course not, but —

MANDY: And he's a really nice guy, Brian. Clever too ... sort of ... Well, Rosie?

[*Pause.*]

ROSIE: I'll think about it, OK?

MANDY: OK, Rosie.

[*'Brass in pocket' by the Pretenders is heard.*]

SCENE EIGHT

ROSIE'*s room.* MANDY *is applying mascara to* ROSIE. *She stops and addresses the audience.*

MANDY: Out on a date? Try 'Lashful' — for lids that allure!
　　[*She turns her attention back to* ROSIE.]

ROSIE: [*uncertainly*] Mandy.

MANDY: Yeah?

ROSIE: D'you reckon this is a good idea?

MANDY: What? The mascara?

ROSIE: No, the whole thing.

MANDY: Sure. Why not?

ROSIE: I don't know, suppose he doesn't like me?

MANDY: [*producing lipstick*] 'Course he will. Hold still!

ROSIE: Not too much!

MANDY: Don't worry. [*Applying a lot*] There.

ROSIE: [*looking in the mirror*] Erk!

MANDY: There's gratitude!

ROSIE: Sorry, Mandy. It's just ... It doesn't look right on me, make up. It looks ... I dunno.

MANDY: Well, you've got to wear it.

ROSIE: Why?

MANDY: You've just got to. And stick some of this on...
　　[*Producing a perfume stick*] Here ... here ... and here.
　　[*She demonstrates on her wrists, her cleavage and in her mouth.*]

ROSIE: [*sniffing the stick*] God, it's revolting!

MANDY: Doesn't matter, it'll turn him on.

ROSIE: Why should I want to turn him on? I've never even seen him. He might be grotesque.

MANDY: He's OK. Anyway, if you get him going, he'll

spread the word that you're hot stuff, and you'll get someone better next time.

ROSIE: Be a lot simpler if girls could ask boys out.

MANDY: Well, you can... if you want to be called a moll!

[*They both smile at the reference.*]

Now stick it on!

[ROSIE *sighs, applies some to her wrists, but stops at her mouth.*]

ROSIE: Why here?

MANDY: For your breath ... For when he kisses you.

ROSIE: Oh, no.

MANDY: Now what?

ROSIE: Suppose *I* don't want to kiss *him*?

MANDY: And have him tell all his mates you're frigid?

ROSIE: He wouldn't.

MANDY: Wouldn't he?

ROSIE: God, what have I let myself in for?

MANDY: Look, there's nothing to worry about. All you've got to do is relax ... and respond.

ROSIE: Respond?

MANDY: Yeah. Only don't come on too strong or you'll scare him off.

ROSIE: Not much risk of that.

MANDY: God, you're funny ... Here, give us that! [*Taking the perfume stick*] Open wide!

[ROSIE *does so, and pokes her tongue out.* MANDY *runs the stick down it.*]

Done.

ROSIE: Yuck!

[*The doorbell rings.*]

That'll be them.

PETER: [*off*] The suckers have arrived.

ROSIE: Shut up, Peter!

PETER: [*poking his head into Rosie's room*] Pardon? [*Seeing* ROSIE] Arrrh! The creature from the black lagoon!

[*He cowers melodramatically.*]

MANDY: Drop dead, junior!

PETER: Well, I mean, she's not seriously going out looking like that, is she?

MANDY: [*warningly*] Peter!

PETER: I suppose she could always put a sack over her head
. . . like 'Elephant Man'.

   [ROSIE *chucks her hairbrush at him.*]

  Hey!

MANDY: Out!

MRS SYMONDS: [*off*] Rosie, your friend's here.

ROSIE: Be down in a minute, Mum. . . [*To* PETER] And if
you dare say a word. . .

MANDY: You look fine, Rosie.

   [ROSIE *looks sceptical*]

  You do!

   [*She goes to take the brush from* PETER. *He holds it
   above his head, out of reach.* MANDY *tries to grab it,
   fails and punches* PETER *hard in the stomach. He
   doubles up. Unconcerned,* MANDY *walks to the door,
   followed by* ROSIE.]

Oh, and remember what I said: don't skate too good.

ROSIE: [*through her teeth*] Mandy!

MANDY: Well, don't forget.

   [*By now they are off.* PETER *staggers after them. Immediately,* MRS SYMONDS *enters through another door,
   followed by* TERRY. *It should appear as though they
   have entered a different room.*]

MRS SYMONDS: There we are, Terry. I'll leave you to it.

   [*She goes.* TERRY *is left alone for a moment. He looks
   around. Through a third entrance,* MANDY *appears
   with* ROSIE.]

MANDY: Hi, Terry . . . Where's Brian?

TERRY: He couldn't make it.

MANDY: Why?

TERRY: I dunno. Just said he couldn't come.

MANDY: But what about Rosie?

   [TERRY *shrugs.*]

  You can still come skating with us, Rosie . . . Can't she,
  Terry?

TERRY: [*without enthusiasm*] Sure.

MANDY: No worries, Rosie.

ROSIE: Thanks, Mandy, but you go. I'd just be in the way.

MANDY: No, you wouldn't.
ROSIE: [*forcefully*] No! I'm not coming, OK? That's final!
    [*Pause*]
MANDY: If you say so, Rosie.
TERRY: [*brightening up*] Well, let's go.
    [MANDY *goes over to him. He puts an arm round her.*]
MANDY: [*turning back at the door*] See you Monday, Rosie?
ROSIE: Yeah . . . See you Monday.
    [*They go, to the sound of 'Haunting' by Carly Simon.*]

SCENE NINE

The Symonds' house. PETER *is on the phone.*

PETER: Yeah, weird! Ever since she got stood up on that
    date . . . Raided the fridge, cleared it out . . . Well, not
    everything. But nearly. Scoffed the lot! . . . Yeah, then
    she stopped again, wouldn't eat a thing . . . Sure, the old
    man used to try and heavy her when he was home, but
    after a couple of tantrums he got pretty jack of it . . .
    [ROSIE *appears, wearing a loose-fitting track suit. She
    overhears* PETER *and, realising that she is the topic of
    conversation, listens unobserved.*]
    . . . Yeah, gave it away. I don't blame him. Oh, and get
    this, this is really crazy: she cooks for us . . . Yeah, two or
    three times a week. Great mountains of food, and she sits
    there with a couple of nuts or something. Really weird!
    [ROSIE *emerges from hiding and walks towards the
    door.*]
ROSIE: [*as she passes* PETER] Don't forget the exercises,
    Peter.
PETER: Eh?
ROSIE: The exercises!
    [*She performs a couple of star jumps.*]
PETER: [*catching on*] Oh, yeah. [*into the phone*] And there's
    the exercises . . . Yeah, she's always doing exercises. Talk
    about a loony —

[ROSIE *grabs the phone and breathes heavily into it before giving it back. She exits.*]

That was her, just going out — running, would you believe! ... I'll tell you something, though: she sure is getting thin!

[*'You can do it' by Richard Simmons is heard.* ACTOR 3, *dressed in a track suit, bounces on.*]

ACTOR 3: [*to the audience*] Yes, thin is in with the active woman of the eighties. For now, more than ever, women are in tune with their feelings and in touch with their bodies. Today's woman both successfully pursues a career *and* raises a family. She radiates both energy and vitality, and her slim, lithe build proclaims to the world that she's fighting fit and going places. So it is not surprising to discover that today's woman is concerned with exercise. She practises jogging ...

[ROSIE *jogs on.*]

Yoga ...

[ROSIE *adopts the 'lion' pose.*]

Callisthenics ...

[ROSIE *demonstrates.*]

Jazz ballet ...

[ROSIE *demonstrates.*]

Disco-cise ...

[ROSIE *demonstrates.*]

Aerobics ...

[*By now,* ROSIE *is begining to weary.*]

Judo ...

[ROSIE *attempts a throw, fails, tries again and collapses.* ACTOR 3 *moves in front of her.*]

Even weight-lifting!

[ROSIE *attempts this while* ACTOR 3 *drums on his knees.* ROSIE *collapses again and stays down.*]

Yes, the list is endless. But one thing today's woman knows is that, if she persists, her sex need never again count against her. For the woman of the eighties, the sky is truly the limit!

[*He jogs off. The music is faded up to cover the change.*]

SCENE TEN

A classroom. ROSIE, MANDY *and* TRISH *are seated.* MR BUTLER, *their teacher, a 'softy', is ending a lesson.*

MR BUTLER: Right, tomorrow, may I remind you, we'll be discussing Henry Handel Richardson's novel, *The Getting of Wisdom* —
   [*Groans and ad-libbed witticisms from* MANDY *and* TRISH.]
   . . . and the particular point we'll be discussing, which I'd like you to be thinking about overnight, will be the one made by er . . .
   [TERRY *enters and* MR BUTLER *continues with relief.*]
   . . . Terry, that Laura (the heroine, I shouldn't have to remind you) is, in Terry's view at any rate, a 'screwed-up, sex-starved Sheila who needed nothing more than a good bloke to sort her out'. That was roughly it, wasn't it, Terry?
TERRY: Something like that, sir.
   [ROSIE *groans.*]
MR BUTLER: Anything the matter, Rosie?
ROSIE: [*affecting boredom*] No, sir.
MR BUTLER: Are you sure?
TERRY: Come on, Rosie, tell us your troubles. Been over-eating again, have you?
ROSIE: Ha, ha.
TERRY: Well, what then?
ROSIE: I thought it would have been obvious, Terry. Even to you.
TRISH: You don't like Terry's topic, right? 'Bout Laura the dag.
ROSIE: A dag? She isn't a dag.
TRISH: Sure she is: daggy and boring.
ROSIE: Crap!
MR BUTLER: Rosie!

TRISH: Oh, dear, I've touched her on a sore spot. Insulted her heroine.

TERRY: Say sorry, then, Trish.

TRISH: Sorry, Rosie.

MR BUTLER: Look, come on you two. If Rosie doesn't approve of Terry's topic, I for one would like to hear why.

ROSIE: Do I have to, sir?

MR BUTLER: If you're going to groan when you hear it read out, then, yes, please!

TERRY: Gotta have the courage of your convictions, Rosie.

TRISH: Yeah.

    [*Pause.*]

ROSIE: OK then, if you really want to know, I think it's crass.

TERRY: Crass?

ROSIE: That's right, Terry, crass.

MR BUTLER: [*intervening quickly*] Er, why's that, Rosie?

ROSIE: Well, 'sex-starved and screwed-up'? I mean: it's a bit puerile, sir.

MR BUTLER: Possibly, but —

TERRY: [*dumbfounded*] Possibly?

MR BUTLER: [*rapidly backpedalling*] Well, yes, as literary criticism goes. But it's still a point. Worth discussing, Rosie.

ROSIE: Is it?

MR BUTLER: Well, it seems to have got you going

ROSIE: But I'm not discussing the point, sir, I'm discussing whether or not we *should* discuss the point. And I don't reckon we should: it's got nothing whatever to do with *The Getting of Wisdom*, and I think talking about it would be a total waste of time.

TERRY: Yeah, like the whole dumb book.

ROSIE: [*crowing*] See! That's his attitude! That's what he really thinks.

TRISH: That's what we *all* think, apart from you, Rosie.

TERRY: Yeah.

MANDY: I don't.

TERRY: What!

MANDY: I don't think it's a waste of time.

TERRY: Oh.

MR BUTLER: Look, I think the best thing would be if, without in any way jeopardising Terry's topic —

TERRY: Eh?

ROSIE: Jeopardise — to put at risk, dummy!

MR BUTLER: . . . we ask Rosie what aspect of the novel she'd prefer us to talk about. Right, Rosie?

TRISH: I know: about what Rosie Symonds has in common with Laura the dag.

MR BUTLER: I'm asking Rosie, Trish.

TERRY: Yeah, about why Rosie Symonds is screwed-up and sex-starved, and why no guy in his right mind would want to sort her out.

MANDY: Shut up, Terry!

TERRY: Well, it's the truth, isn't it?

TRISH: That's right, Mandy. Anyone with half a mind could work out why she's so stoked on the book. She's got the same hang-ups that Laura had.

ROSIE: But Laura hasn't got hang-ups.

TRISH: Oh, no?

ROSIE: No! It's everyone else in the book that's got the hang-ups. Laura's the only one with the guts to be herself.

TERRY: Just like you, eh?

TRISH: Yeah, one freak admiring another.

ROSIE: That's not being a freak: having the guts to be different! Having the guts to be yourself! God, look at you two: you're so *ordinary*. Whatever you're told to do, you do it. Some crumby magazine or pop-star says look like this, dress like this, do this — and you do! Exactly what you're told to do! . . . And do you know why! Eh! D'you know why?

TERRY: Why?

ROSIE: Because you've been *brainwashed*, that's why!

TERRY: But at least we're not freaks.

MR BUTLER: Now, come on.

TRISH: Or weirdos.

MR BUTLER: Stop this!

TERRY: [*leaping to his feet*] And anyway, what right's she got to talk about anyone else being brainwashed, sir? I mean, that bloke who writes those Weight-Watchers ads has sure got through to her. Hasn't he, *Bones*?

MANDY: [*also standing*] Shut your mouth, Terry!

TERRY: What?

MANDY: I said *shut it* — you creep!

MR BUTLER: [*shouting*] All right!

> [*Pause.* TERRY *and* MANDY *confront one another eye-ball to eyeball. Eventually,* TERRY *resumes his seat, then* MANDY *hers.* MR BUTLER *attempts to regain control.*]

Well, I don't know what to say . . . Tomorrow, we'll talk about Terry's point, and the point that seems to have developed out of what Rosie said — about Laura as an outsider. And I trust we'll all be able to exert a bit more self-control than we did today. I'll see you then.

> [*He goes, quickly. The others start to clear up their things.* TERRY *gets up to leave. He turns by the door.*]

TERRY: Oh, Mandy, before I go . . .

MANDY: Yeah?

TERRY: [*in a hard voice*] Don't call me a creep again. Ever! Understand?

> [*Pause.*]

Coming, Trish?

TRISH: Sure, Terry.

> [*She follows him dutifully to the door. They leave.* MANDY *thinks for a moment, then follows and yells through the door after them.*]

MANDY: Great creep!

> [*She waits, but* TERRY *does not return. She goes over to* ROSIE.]

Don't know what I ever saw in him.

ROSIE: Oh, well . . .

> [*She turns back to packing her case.*]

MANDY: You all right, Rosie?

ROSIE: [*disdainfully*] 'Course I'm all right.

MANDY: [*unperturbed*] Want to come for coffee?

ROSIE: [*warming a little*] Thanks, Mandy, but I've got to go home . . . Really! I'm cooking.

MANDY: Make them wait.

ROSIE: I can't. Dad's getting back from some business trip.

So I said I'd cook.

MANDY: I wish you'd eat something yourself.

ROSIE: [*sharply*] Now don't you start, Mandy, please. I get enough of that at home.

MANDY: OK.

ROSIE: Anyway, I eat plenty.

MANDY: OK.

   [*Pause.*]

Well, take care, Rosie.

   [*She looks at her affectionately.*]

ROSIE: Don't worry about me, Mandy. I will.

   [MANDY *looks unconvinced.*]

   I *will.*

   [*Romantic music is heard.* ACTOR 4 *enters as* MANDY *exits. He is wearing a smoking jacket and smokes a cheroot.*]

ACTOR 4: [*to audience*] I *will,* the latest in a long line of romantic novels from the pen of best-selling woman's author, Barbara Cartland. In this thrilling tale of high passion, handsome rugged cosmetic surgeon, Terry Burns [*endowing himself with the part*] meets the woman of his dreams, petite and beautiful Patricia Knight. [*Endowing* ROSIE *with the part*] He proposes marriage [*pulling* ROSIE *down on to his knee*], only to discover that his bride-to-be has cancer of the breast.

   [*They look; horror*]

Will our hero save his intended's life *and* her curvaceous little figure? Will he be able to fix it so that she still has a bosom to heave gently on her wedding day as she murmurs the magic words . . .

   [*He looks at* ROSIE. *She is immobile. He shakes her.*]

ROSIE: I will.

ACTOR 4: Read *I Will,* a woman's novel for today!

   [*The music swells to cover the scene change.*]

SCENE ELEVEN

The Symonds dining room. MR *and* MRS SYMONDS *are in the middle of an argument.*

MR SYMONDS: Well, I'm worried, even if you're not.
MRS SYMONDS: Of course I'm worried.
MR SYMONDS: Coming back, seeing her after a month —
MRS SYMONDS: Well, maybe if you hadn't been away —
MR SYMONDS: That's right: blame me!
MRS SYMONDS: I'm not blaming you, George —
PETER: [*off*] Grub up, yet?
MR SYMONDS: We'll talk about this later.
MRS SYMONDS: Why not now?
MR SYMONDS: [*glancing off, in* PETER*'s direction*] You know
  very well why!
MRS SYMONDS: And what about Rosie?
MR SYMONDS: You've had it your way. Now it's my turn.
  [PETER *enters.*]
PETER: Er . . . excuse me?
MR SYMONDS: [*sharply*] Yes?
  [ROSIE *enters bearing two plates.*]
ROSIE: Here we are.
PETER: Nothing, Dad. Question answered.
  [*They all sit down.* ROSIE *puts the plates in her parents'
  places, then she exits.*]
MR SYMONDS: [*looking after her*] It's not natural . . . and it
  should never have been allowed to go this far.
  [ROSIE *re-appears with two more plates and puts one
  down in front of* PETER.]
ROSIE: Peter.
  [*She puts the remaining plate in her own place and sits
  down. No one moves.* ROSIE *looks round in conster-
  nation.*]
  Well, you may begin.
  [PETER *goes to pick up his knife and fork, but his father*

stops him with a gesture.]

MR SYMONDS: Rosie, before we eat, I want to ask you something.

[*Pause.*]

ROSIE: [*uneasily*] Yes, Dad?

MR SYMONDS: [*after a look at his wife*] How much do you weigh?

ROSIE: What. Dad?

MR SYMONDS: How much, Rosie, do you weigh?

ROSIE: [*nervously*] Funny question.

MR SYMONDS: Never mind about that. Just answer it!

ROSIE: Why?

MR SYMONDS: Why!

MRS SYMONDS: Because we're worried about you, Rosie.

MR SYMONDS: Well, look at you . . . and look at what you're eating.

ROSIE: Health food.

MR SYMONDS: Health food! Your plate's nearly empty.

ROSIE: So? I'm not a slave to my appetite.

MR SYMONDS: You don't seem to have an appetite.

[*Pause.*]

ROSIE: Don't let your food go cold.

MR SYMONDS: [*shouting*] Rosie! How much do you weigh?

ROSIE: [*shouting back*] Thirty-nine and a half kilograms.

MR SYMONDS: Not in those things, in stones.

ROSIE: [*contemptuously*] I have no idea.

MR SYMONDS: Peter, get the scales, please.

PETER: Dad?

MR SYMONDS: Get the scales!

PETER: [*shrugging*] OK.

[*He goes.*]

ROSIE: [*wearily*] Do we have to go through all this on your first night back? I mean it's not as though I'm wasting food, or throwing Mum's cooking back in her face, is it?

PETER: [*off*] They're not in the bathroom, Dad.

[MR SYMONDS *looks at his wife, who shouts back to* PETER.]

MRS SYMONDS: They must be. Look a bit harder!

PETER: [*re-appearing*] Well, they're not . . . Hang on, I've got an idea.

  [*He looks meaningfully at* ROSIE, *and exits again.*]

  [*off*] Got them!

  [*He re-appears carrying the bathroom scales. He brings them to his father, who points to the place on the floor where they are to go.* PETER *puts them down and sits.* MR SYMONDS *gets up and walks over to the scales.*]

MR SYMONDS: Now, Rosie.

  [ROSIE *walks over to the scales. She hesitates, and then gets on.* MR SYMONDS *bends over to read the weight. He is horrified.*]

Six stone two pounds.

  [ROSIE *steps off.*]

She weighed more than that when she was twelve.

ROSIE: [*calmly*] Can we get on with dinner now, please?

  [*She starts to walk back to her place, but her father catches her by the arm and spins her round. He speaks to her with great urgency.*]

MR SYMONDS: Now look, Rosie, I don't know what's going on, but it's nearly a year since you started this . . . slimming business. And I've watched you wasting away, and let you get away with it. But now I'm putting my foot down. You're going to see a doctor, Rosie. If I have to drag you there myself, you are.

  [ROSIE *looks at her mother for support.*]

MRS SYMONDS: He means it, Rosie.

  [*Pause.*]

ROSIE: OK, Dad. But I'll go by myself. All right?

MR SYMONDS: But you will go?

ROSIE: I said OK, didn't I? . . . Now, can we eat?

MR SYMONDS: [*ironically*] Can we eat?

  [ROSIE, MR SYMONDS *and* PETER *freeze at the table as* ACTOR 2 *rises and addresses the audience in her role as* 'Super-Mum'.]

ACTOR 2: And the answer to that question is: Yes, we can, with *The Australian Women's Weekly Cookbook.* [*Displaying a copy*] Here you will find many mouth-watering recipes from the weekly features, as well as new and exciting dishes that you will just love to cook for your

family over and over . . . and over and over . . . and over
and over . . . and over and over and over and over and
over and over . . . again.
  ['*Walking on Thin Ice*' *by Yoko Ono is heard.*]

SCENE TWELVE

Doctor Morris's surgery. The DOCTOR, *who is elderly and
Scottish, is summing up.*

DOCTOR: So, Rosie, you're not sleeping too well, you're feel-
  ing a bit listless and you'd like some sleeping pills and
  some tonic?
ROSIE: [*In a small voice*] Yes, doctor.
DOCTOR: No other problems?
ROSIE: No.
DOCTOR: Your periods: are they normal, regular?
ROSIE: Oh, a bit irregular.
DOCTOR: You look a bit peaky. Are you eating properly?
ROSIE: Oh, yes. Fine.
DOCTOR: I think we'll just pop you on the scales anyway.
ROSIE: [*suddenly jumpy*] Oh, no. There's no need. I'm fine.
  Forty-six kilos. I weighed myself last night.
DOCTOR: Well, you're a little underweight for your age and
  height, but nothing to worry about . . . if your scales were
  accurate, that is.
ROSIE: [*hurriedly*] Oh, yes. They're accurate.
DOCTOR: Had them checked, have you?
ROSIE: [*agitatedly*] Yes, I . . . Dad did.
DOCTOR: [*humorously*] Well, we can double-check them if
  you like. See if they give the same reading as my trusty old
  beam balance.
ROSIE: No, thanks, Doctor Morris.
DOCTOR: Well, have it your way. I'll just write you your
  prescription.
    [*He reaches for the pad and starts to write. His manner
    as he speaks is offhand.*]

There is — just by the way — one disease that involves young girls losing weight rapidly, a kind of self-starvation disease. But I don't suppose for a moment you've got it — probably just worry about exams and so forth in your case, getting you run down a bit, eh?

ROSIE: Suppose so, doctor.

DOCTOR: [*handing the prescription over*] Hmm. Can be quite nasty, this disease. Quite often starts off with slimming, and after a while, the . . . victim finds that she can't stop slimming. She eats less and less, and loses more and more weight, and the one thing that really seems to terrify her is putting on weight again . . . You've not had any such feelings, I suppose, Rosie?

ROSIE: No, doctor.

DOCTOR: You've never felt, for example, that by not eating, you're somehow controlling an aspect of your life that no one else can control? . . . Kind of going on a hunger strike?

ROSIE: No . . . I'm not a member of the I.R.A., doctor.

DOCTOR: No, of course not . . . Still, it is a curious disease. You know, girls who have it, even when not eating starts to harm them physically, they usually carry on with it. At first, I gather, they tend to feel very active and energetic: you know, in control of themselves. But when their weight drops by round about twenty per cent — that would be down to about . . . forty three kilos in your case, Rosie — their periods stop. Oh, they still might feel fine for a while. But not for long! They gradually grow weaker, more . . . listless. They begin to suffer from insomnia. And, of course, they start to get scared! But curiously enough, they still won't eat, many of them. And what this does to the body, as you might imagine, can be very serious, if not permanent. In fact, it can kill them!

   [*Pause.*]

Well, you've got your prescription, Rosie.

ROSIE: Thank you, doctor.

   [*She takes it and stands. As she is about to leave, the* DOCTOR *continues.*]

DOCTOR: Oh, by the way, just for the record I should tell

you that there is treatment available for people with this disease I've been talking about. But, oddly enough, an awful lot of girls who get it don't want to be helped. They prefer to pretend that there's nothing wrong with them. Even to themselves. They get very secretive, tell terrible lies . . . You could say, I suppose, that they choose to commit suicide slowly.

[*Pause.*]

ROSIE: Why are you telling me this, doctor? . . . I haven't got this disease, you know.

DOCTOR: Then let me put you on the scales.

ROSIE: I told you —

DOCTOR: OK, have it your way. You say you're fine —

ROSIE: And, anyway, suppose I did only weigh forty-three kilos — would I have it? Definitely?

DOCTOR: Not necessarily.

[*Pause.*]

ROSIE: Well, what about . . . forty kilos?

DOCTOR: That's very low, Rosie.

ROSIE: But would I have it?

[*Pause.*]

DOCTOR: You seem very concerned.

ROSIE: I'd just like to know . . . for the record.

DOCTOR: Well . . . I'd say, probably.

[*Pause.*]

ROSIE: And how would you know, definitely?

DOCTOR: Well, when did you say your last period was?

ROSIE: I didn't.

DOCTOR: Then tell me now.

[*Pause.*]

ROSIE: Five months ago.

[*Pause.*]

DOCTOR: In that case, I think you know the answer to your own question.

[ROSIE *sits.*]

ROSIE: Well . . . So what happens now?

DOCTOR: I'm going to make a referral, Rosie. To a psychiatrist. And if she can't get you to eat . . . it'll be hospital, I'm afraid.

ROSIE: Hospital?

DOCTOR: Well, let's hope it doesn't come to that. Eh?
  [*The final (shout) sequence of 'Walking on Thin Ice' is
  heard.*]

SCENE THIRTEEN

The psychiatric ward of a large hospital. MR *and* MRS
SYMONDS *enter, shown in by a* PSYCHIATRIST.

PSYCHIATRIST: If you'd wait here please, while Rosie gets
  changed. Then you can have a few minutes to say good-
  bye to her.

MR SYMONDS: [*coldly*] Thank you.
  [*The* PSYCHIATRIST *leaves.*]
  God, what have we done?

MRS SYMONDS: How do you mean, George?

MR SYMONDS: How do I mean? This bloody place is crawling
  with loonies! Haven't you seen them?

MRS SYMONDS: Well, it is a psychiatric ward, so . . .

MR SYMONDS: My daughter in a nut-house! Well, no wonder
  she was crying all the way here.

MRS SYMONDS: But if staying here does the trick? If it cures
  her —

MR SYMONDS: Cures her! Why should it? Why the hell
  should she eat in here any better than in any other ward of
  the hospital? Or is sharing a trough with loonies supposed
  to sharpen her appetite somehow?

MRS SYMONDS: Perhaps they want her in this ward so they
  can . . . discover what's wrong with her mind.

MR SYMONDS: There you go again: talking about her as
  though she's demented or —

MRS SYMONDS: Not demented, George, but . . . well, you've
  got to admit that something's not right.

MR SYMONDS: Sure! But not with her mind.

MRS SYMONDS: Well, what then?

MR SYMONDS: I don't know: attention-seeking, some stupid

teenage rebellion.

MRS SYMONDS: Well, whatever it is, you don't know how to stop it!

[*Slight pause.*]

MR SYMONDS: Maybe not. But do they? Does that girl she's been with for the past three months?

MRS SYMONDS: Her psychiatrist?

MR SYMONDS: Yes, of course, her! Terrific success she's had! Rosie's worse now than when she started with her.

MRS SYMONDS: Well, maybe if she'd had a bit more co-operation —

MR SYMONDS: What do you mean: more co-operation? Do you mean that just because I wouldn't have a bar of her so-called 'family-sessions' . . .

[MRS SYMONDS *looks away.*]

All right, why? Give me one reason why I should have let that girl pry into our affairs.

MRS SYMONDS: Well, if it could possibly have helped Rosie —

MR SYMONDS: If I thought for one minute that it could possible have helped Rosie, then of course I would have agreed to it. But *how* could it? How could it have helped?

MRS SYMONDS: Perhaps if something in the family was . . . causing the upset —

MR SYMONDS: Then Rosie's had ample opportunity to tell her herself. And I'm damned if I can see how getting the whole family to sit round in a circle and bombarding us with a lot of personal questions about our private affairs could possibly have told her any more . . . Anyway, why should it be something in the family? What the hell's wrong with us that's not wrong with any damn family?

MRS SYMONDS: That's what the psychiatrist might have found out, George.

[MR SYMONDS *is prevented from replying by the entry of the* PSYCHIATRIST.]

PSYCHIATRIST: Well, she seems to be settling down now, getting used to the idea of being here for a bit.

[MRS SYMONDS *nods.*]

She should be with you in a minute.

[*The* PSYCHIATRIST *is about to leave when there is a
disturbance off-stage.*]

FEMALE PATIENT: [*off*] Don't want to, don't want to, don't
want to . . .

MALE NURSE: [*off*] Now come on, Nancy. Come on, come
on!

    [*Silence.* MR *and* MRS SYMONDS *look concerned. The*
PSYCHIATRIST *turns to them.*]

PSYCHIATRIST: Some of the patients can be a bit awkward at
times.

MR SYMONDS: Yes, we noticed some of them . . . [*exchang-
ing a look with his wife*] and, quite honestly, it made us
wonder what Rosie was doing in the same ward.

    [*Slight pause.*]

PSYCHIATRIST: Well, I can understand your concern, Mr
Symonds, but frankly, I do find it a bit surprising —

MR SYMONDS: What?

PSYCHIATRIST: . . . surprising that you don't know why
Rosie's here.

MR SYMONDS: [*astounded*] You what?

PSYCHIATRIST: Well, you've been living in the same house as
her. So I can't seriously accept that you haven't noticed
that something's been wrong.

MR SYMONDS: Yes, but —

PSYCHIATRIST: Of course, I realise that it must have been
pretty scary for you to watch your daughter starving
herself to death —

MR SYMONDS: Now, come on —

PSYCHIATRIST: . . . because that's exactly what's been happening, Mr Symonds. Isn't it?

MR SYMONDS: [*shaken*] Now, look, obviously I know that
Rosie's not been eating —

PSYCHIATRIST: And she's been forcing herself to vomit,
taking vast quantities of laxatives and slimming pills,
exercising frantically. She's been in acute emotional tur-
moil —

MR SYMONDS: All right! I've agreed that something's wrong
. . . OK, very wrong.

PSYCHIATRIST: So why does it surprise you that she's been

admitted to a psychiatric ward?

MR SYMONDS: [*weakly*] But if all you're going to do is get her to eat —

PSYCHIATRIST: *All?* Are you seriously suggesting that it's going to be easy?

MR SYMONDS: Well, no, I don't suppose —

PSYCHIATRIST: I've already been working with Rosie for three months, don't forget.

MR SYMONDS: Yes, all right, I know! But what makes us, well, concerned is that we still haven't been told what's wrong with her, and —

PSYCHIATRIST: She's not eating.

MR SYMONDS: We know that —

PSYCHIATRIST: Right. You know as much as I do, then.

[*Pause.*]

Look, Mr Symonds, if it would make you any happier, I could let you have a whole bunch of theories that try to explain why some girls choose to become anorexic rather than grow up into fully functioning women. But they're very general theories. There might be a lot of truth in them, and they might go some way towards explaining what's wrong with our society. But they don't tell me why one girl becomes anorexic and another one doesn't.

MR SYMONDS: So how do you find that out?

PSYCHIATRIST: Well, as I told you before, ideally I'd like to spend some time with the whole family, but if that's not to be —

[ROSIE *enters in a dressing-gown. The* PSYCHIATRIST *breaks off.*]

ROSIE: [*in a small frightened voice*] Hello.

PSYCHIATRIST: [*warmly*] Hello, Rosie.

[MRS SYMONDS *goes over to* ROSIE. *She sits her down.*]

MR SYMONDS: [*to* PSYCHIATRIST] 'If that's not to be'?

PSYCHIATRIST: Then, when all else fails, it has to be hospitalisation.

[ROSIE *and* MRS SYMONDS *listen to this conversation.*]

MR SYMONDS: In the psychiatric ward?

PSYCHIATRIST: Well, that's where I work.

MR SYMONDS: [*grimly*] In with the loonies.

PSYCHIATRIST: If you like — in with the loonies.
  [*Pause.*]
MR SYMONDS: So that's the kind of ultimatum you're pre-
  pared to hold over me, is it?
PSYCHIATRIST: I'm sorry?
MR SYMONDS: Either I agree to these family ordeals of yours
  or you subject my daughter to this.
MRS SYMONDS: **George!**
PSYCHIATRIST: Not at all, Mr Symonds. If you want to dis-
  charge Rosie and seek alternative treatment, that's fine by
  me.
MR SYMONDS: [*surprised*] Is it?
PSYCHIATRIST: Sure. It's not going to do Rosie any good to
  hold her against her will. Or the will of her family.
  [*Pause.*]
MR SYMONDS: Well, you'd better get dressed then, Rosie.
MRS SYMONDS: No, George.
MR SYMONDS: What?
MRS SYMONDS: We can't just take Rosie home.
MRS SYMONDS: Why not? . . . Look, what are they going to
  do with her here? Keep her in bed and insist she eat her
  . . . however many calories it is —
PSYCHIATRIST: [*helpfully*] Three thousand.
MR SYMONDS: Three thousand. Every day, right? And not
  give her any privileges unless she does. No visitors, no
  books, no TV, nothing. Right? . . . Well, we could do all
  that at home. Easily! Couldn't we, Rosie? That'd be bet-
  ter, wouldn't it?
MRS SYMONDS: But it's not happening, George.
MR SYMONDS: Look, I'm not arguing with you —
MRS SYMONDS: But *I* am arguing.
MR SYMONDS: Well, don't, please!
MRS SYMONDS: George, listen!
MR SYMONDS: Mary!
MRS SYMONDS: George! As you know yourself, this has gone
  on for over a year —
MR SYMONDS: Mary!
MRS SYMONDS: *Will you let me speak!*
  [*There is an embarrassed pause.* MRS SYMONDS

resumes.]

Right. It's been going on for over a year, *with* Rosie at home. And we've got nowhere. Nowhere!

MR SYMONDS: Largely because you've been too damn soft.

MRS SYMONDS: I've been soft, you've been away —

MR SYMONDS: I wondered when that was coming: 'I've been away'.

MRS SYMONDS: Well, you are hardly ever home, George.

MR SYMONDS: Yes, and you know why too. You know what happens if I don't put in the hours. To my position in the firm.

MRS SYMONDS: But it's your position in the family that we're talking about —

MR SYMONDS: Well, it does rather affect my position in the family if I get the sack, you know. Since I am the only breadwinner.

MRS SYMONDS: Through no fault of mine.

MR SYMONDS: What?

MRS SYMONDS: Through no fault of mine! D'you think I wouldn't have loved to have a career? To have done something with my life. Instead of just keeping house for you?

MR SYMONDS: Well, this is the first I've heard of it.

MRS SYMONDS: Nonsense!

MR SYMONDS: It's not nonsense —

MRS SYMONDS: I've told you a thousand times —

MR SYMONDS: OK, then, go out tomorrow. Get a job! You can take over! Great!

MRS SYMONDS: Don't be stupid, George! How can I simply go out and get a job? I've had no education, no training, no experience. I gave all that up when I —

[*She suddenly realises what she's saying, breaks off and turns round to look at* ROSIE, *who is sitting withdrawn and frightened and on the verge of tears.* MR SYMONDS *also turns to look at her. He turns back to his wife. There is a rare moment of understanding between them.*]

God, George, what have we done?

[*Pause. Suddenly there is a trumpet fanfare.* ACTOR 4

enters. He pulls ROSIE *stage centre. The rest of the cast line up, two each side of her. They address the audience.*]

ACTOR 4: Would you like to be your own person? Free from the pressures of parents!

ACTOR 5: Boyfriends!

ACTOR 4: Girlfriends!

ACTOR 3: Sex!

ACTOR 2: Clothes!

ACTOR 5: Make-up!

ACTOR 3: Growing up!

ACTOR 4: TV!

ACTOR 5: Unemployment!

ACTOR 2: The future!

ACTOR 4: Then anorexia nervosa could be a way for you! It's so cheap to stop eating. The most it can cost you...

   [*All freeze.* ROSIE'*s head falls to her chest.*]

... is your life.

   [*All turn their heads to look at* ROSIE. *Pause. She raises her head and steps smartly back into line. All bow.*]

THE END

Hey Mum, I Own a Factory!

Magpie Theatre-in-Education Company

State Theatre Company of South Australia

Helene Burden, Kelvin Harman, Maree Cochrane and Caroline Baker in the Magpie Theatre-in-Education Company production of *Hey Mum, I Own a Factory!* Photo by David Wilson.

FOREWORD

This play is suitable for performance to upper year high school students and beyond to a general adult audience. Why should theatre-in-education only be for school children after all!

Hey Mum I Own a Factory! was written and presented by the Magpie company because of constant requests from teachers for a play about unemployment. Rather than do a play about *unemployment*, the company decided to do a play about *employment*. The difference between the two is as important as the difference in real life. One is a positive, the other a negative experience. One provides the means for a livelihood and some sort of creative expression, the other creates the social role of 'unperson'. There has always been a tendency in didactic theatre to *tell* the audience how grim the world is. My own response to such a message is usually depression and immobility and this is exactly what I observed among youth audiences when faced with the usual offerings on the subject of unemployment. The reality young people face is quite bad enough. Therefore, Magpie presented a play about employment — with an interesting twist.

In the early Seventies, a group of women in South Australia took over the factory in which they worked, after the owners had closed it down. With this event as the kernel of an idea, the story of *Hey Mum* ... was conceived and written and peopled by characters plucked from the collective mind and experience of the company.

The story fulfilled an important criterion for me: that theatre-in-education had to move away from issue-generated work, to work based on close observation of life, from which issues would naturally arise. That is to say, there had to be more writing from life than writing to an idea. The issues which arose from this particular story were many: employment, capitalist work relationships, cooperative work, pink-collar industries, the traditional roles of men and women workers and the right of married women to work. The latter at the time was particularly important because there had been a vociferous national campaign against married women working.

Of great importance also was the fact that the story described how hitherto ordinary, quiet, working women took an active part in the creation of their own histories. They showed how the world could be changed by changing their own situation.

There was criticism from some that the effect of the play was undermined by the failure of the women's project in the end. However, the company felt that dramatically, the major point of the story was the concept of taking personal responsibility. In this way we were able to illustrate clearly the women's problems. We all learn from mistakes; error, unfortunately, being the best teacher.

The genesis of the play is of interest because it is the product of ten people working closely together — the cast, the designer, the company writer/researcher and Doreen Clark who at the time was the writer-in-residence with the State Theatre Co. of S.A. of which Magpie is an integral part. Doreen helped to reshape the dialogue.

It is in particular reference to the leaden porridge of social realist theatre, that one hears the cliché: plays can't be written by committees. They can be, but they are usually terrible. However, I believe this play is a good one and it was made by a group. The method, therefore, is instructive.

Along with the basic story outline, detailed research was provided to all company members by the company writer/researcher. Numerous people helped with research, including trade unionists and academics such as Ray Jureidini of Flinders University, whose study of cooperatives was most useful. Along with two members of the cast, the writer/researcher interviewed various working women and together with the whole company, trekked around factories in Adelaide gaining the willing cooperation of many, many people.

On the basis of all this work, character improvisations were undertaken. Each actor was able to build up his or her character according to the agreed guidelines which we had arrived at after group discussion. The actors were all particularly skilled in this kind of improvisatory work, and from this came some lovely characters like Marilyn Allen's Vi, and Helene Burden's Collette, both pivotal characters.

So the play grew in a controlled, organic way. This was possible because the proper groundwork had been laid. Group written plays often lack this preparation. Fortunately, our group worked very well together — another vital ingredient.

After the performance of the play in each school, various methods were used in discussing the work with the audience. At times teachers would organise debates. At other times, each actor, in character, would enter what we called the 'hot-seat', to be attacked, praised and generally cross-examined by the audience. This is a testing time for any actor and character. Given the work our actors had put in, they had no difficulty handling these moments, which were in themselves quite fascinating.

Hey Mum . . . is a play which presents a positive alternative to the usual manner of focussing on unemployment.

John Lonie, December 1984

Hey Mum, I Own a Factory! was first performed by the Magpie Theatre-in-Education Company at the Playhouse, Adelaide Festival Centre on 11 April 1981 with the following cast:

VI GRIFFITHS	Marilyn Allen
DI HARRIS	Caroline Baker
CONNIE DYER MRS MANDERS	Maree Cochrane
HARRY NAYLOR REG DOUGHERTY EDDIE GRIFFITHS	Kelvin Harman
COLETTE MANDERS	Helene Burden
BOB DYER TED SPENCE	Geoff Revell

Directed by Malcolm Moore
Designed by Ken Wilby
Writer/Researcher, John Lonie

CHARACTERS

VI GRIFFITHS, forewoman, 42 years old
CONNIE DYER, leading hand, 32 years old
DI HARRIS, machinist, 28 years old
COLETTE MANDERS, junior, 16 years old
MRS MANDERS, housewife, 38 years old
HARRY NAYLOR, manager of Protectaware, 47 years old
TED SPENCE, maintenance and store supervisor, 32 years old
REG DOUGHERTY, secretary of the Australian Textile Workers Union, 40 years old
EDDIE GRIFFITHS, Vi's husband, 45 years old
BOB DYER, Connie's husband, 35 years old

SETTING

Most of the action takes place in the Protectaware factory. A raised section of the stage represents the office, which has a large calendar and a clock on the wall.

The lower part of the stage represents the factory floor and the canteen.

Other scenes take place in the homes of the workers.

HEY MUM, I OWN A FACTORY!

SCENE ONE

The factory. The calendar reads September and the clock is at seven-thirty. The siren sounds. NAYLOR *enters with cards and stands on the step leading to the office. As each woman enters she takes a card from* NAYLOR, *clocks in and goes to her machine.*

NAYLOR: My name is Harry Naylor and I'm the manager of this factory. We produce protective leatherware for industry.
[VI *enters.*]
Vi Griffiths. Vi's been with us for nine years. She is the forewoman and union rep.
[CONNIE *enters.*]
Connie Dyer, machine operator and leading hand. Been with us for seven years.
[DI *enters.*]
Di Harris. Machine operator. Two-and-a-half years.
[TED SPENCE *enters.* NAYLOR *hands him his card.* TED *clocks in and exits.*]
Ted Spence. Maintenance and store supervisor. Three years' service.
[COLETTE *enters.*]
Colette Manders.
[*He directs* COLETTE *into his office. He follows and they sit.*]
Come in, Colette, take a seat. Now, Colette, have you ever worked in a factory before?

SCENE TWO

Machine noise starts. The women unfreeze and start working.

VI: [*over the machine noise*] What are you up to now, Connie?

CONNIE: [*checking numbers*] Oh . . . about eighty-nine, Vi.

VI: Try and speed it up a bit, love. We're a bit behind with the quota.

CONNIE: Oh, there's something the matter with this feeder.

VI: Not again. I'll have to get Spence onto it. Ted! Ted!

TED: [*off*] Yeah. What's the problem, Vi?

VI: It's this flaming feeder on number two again. The one you said you'd fixed.

TED: [*off*] Have you tried a bit of oil?
  [TED *enters.*]

VI: [*to* CONNIE] I could oil me fingernails, but they wouldn't move any faster. [*To* TED] Have another look at it, will you?
  [TED *goes to look.*]
Not now; when they've finished.
  [TED *scowls and looks as if he is going to argue.*]

NAYLOR: [*off*] Vi, could you come up to my office? Now, please.

VI: Right, Mr. Naylor. [*To* TED] Leave it. You can see to it after.
  [*She exits.*]

TED: [*to* DI] What does the boss want with Vi?

DI: I dunno, Ted love.
  [VI *enters with* COLETTE.]

VI: Well, this is it. The factory floor. There are forty-two women that work here. This is Colette, girls; she'll be with you lot.

CONNIE: Isn't she lucky?

VI: Now, Connie, you wouldn't know what to do with yourself if you didn't come here every day.

CONNIE: I only come for the wages.

DI: Don't we all?

TED: I'm Mr Spence.

VI: Oh, this is Ted.

TED: I manage the storeroom and organise the running of the orders.

VI: [*sotto voce*] That's about all he does get running. He's a dead loss when it comes to the machines.

TED: [*overhearing*] Damn it, Vi. It's not my fault. Spare parts for those old machines are as scarce as hen's teeth.

VI: All right, Ted. Go and crow in your own barnyard. You're in the road in here. [*To* COLETTE, *indicating* DI] You'll be on the small gloves line with these girls here. These two do the last bits.

> [NAYLOR *moves the clock to ten. Siren. The girls go to the canteen*]

The hard bits. We'll train you on this machine here on the easy bits. In your spare time you run round making sure every girl has a good supply of fresh parts from the cutting press. Then she doesn't have to stop sewing. That hooter was for tea break. You get two. Ten minutes in the morning at ten, and then at two-thirty. Start work at seven-thirty. A half-hour for lunch. Finish at four. Don't look so worried. There's always pay day. Come on, I'll introduce you to the girls.

CONNIE: Here comes the old duck with the new girl.

VI: This here's Connie. She's the leading mouth, I mean hand.

CONNIE: Hello, Colette. It is Colette, isn't it?

COLETTE: Yeah.

CONNIE: Come and sit down. We'll look after you.

VI: And this is Di.

DI: Coffee?

> [*All reply in the affirmative.* DI *hands round the coffee.*]

VI: Thanks, Di. [*To* CONNIE] How's Bob?

CONNIE: Working hard. Back's still playing up.

VI: Too much Saturday Night Fever.

CONNIE: Wish it was.
COLETTE: [*with blatant disbelief*] Do you go to discos?
     [*They all laugh.*]
VI: Connie and Bob are both too tired through the week,
     love, so they have a bit of a rave-up on Saturday nights.
COLETTE: Oh.
CONNIE: We all know Eddie's limit. Once a month if you're
     lucky, isn't it, Vi?
VI: Yeah, and it's him who lies back and thinks of England
     and I have to do all the flaming work. [*To* COLETTE]
     Don't take any notice of us, love. Is your dad up at the
     works, then?
COLETTE: Nah. Works at the bakery. Night shift.
VI: What about your mum?
COLETTE: Oh, she doesn't work. She's just a housewife.
VI: You the only one or . . . ?
COLETTE: Two kid brothers. Both at school. Is it all married
     women in here?
DI: I was, but Sam shot through on us.
CONNIE: You haven't heard from him? Must be all of twelve
     months?
DI: Nah. He'll be up in Darwin by now. Deserters' retreat.
     Hope the crocs get him. Me and the kids are hardly likely
     to see him again.
CONNIE: You've always got Ted.
VI: Yeah, if she can catch him. You got a boy friend,
     Colette?
COLETTE: Sort of. He's . . .
     [NAYLOR *puts the clock to ten-ten and sounds the siren.*
     The girls leave.]
VI: Connie, show Colette the lockers, will you. [*To* COL-
     ETTE] Right. See you tomorrow, then? Bright and early.
COLETTE: Oh, right, yeah. Thanks, Vi. [VI *puts clock to*
     three-thirty. TED *comes in and clocks off.*]
VI: Hey, where are you off to?
TED: Got a dental appointment.
VI: I thought you were going to fix that machine?
TED: I can't, I've looked in the storeroom and there's
     nothing to fix it with.

VI: Honestly, Ted, you give me the willies. How am I sup-
   posed to get the quotas out if you can't fix the machines?
TED: You'll have to fix them yourself next week. 'Cos I'm
   leaving.
VI: I've heard that before.
TED: This time I mean it. I'm setting up on my own.
VI: Your own boss? You'll like that.
TED: Well, some of us can and some of us can't.
   [*He moves off.*]
VI: And some of us only think they can.
   [VI *moves the clock to four. Siren.* VI *and* DI *clock off.*
   DI *goes.*]
DI: Night, Vi.
VI: Night, love.
CONNIE: [*off*] Night, Vi.
VI: Night, Connie.
NAYLOR: [*going*] Night, Vi.
VI: Night, Mr Naylor.
   [*She goes.*]

SCENE THREE

---

*The Manders' family home. There is a confused noise of kids
screaming, a dog barking, the television blaring, taps running, etc.*

MUM: [*off*] Scott, will you do as you're told for once and get
   that bike out of the way so's your Dad can get his car in.
   Craig! Have you seen Craig? Where is that kid. Craig
   Manders! Get down off that roof. No. NOW. Your bath's
   ready. Oh! The bath!
   [*A dog yelps.*]
Stupid dog.
   [MUM *enters and stands tearing her hair.*]
I've had you lot. You wait until your father comes home.
Just you wait.
   [COLETTE *enters.*]

COLETTE: Mum.

MUM: Where the hell have you been? Where's the bread?

COLETTE: Oh . . . I forgot. Mum . . .

MUM: Can't you do the one little thing I ask you?

COLETTE: Mum, I've got a job.

MUM: I'm sick to death of running around after you lot. Now how am I going to make your father's lunch up?

COLETTE: At the leather factory.

MUM: If you want anything done you gotta —
What did you say?

COLETTE: I've got a job. I thought you'd be pleased?

MUM: Oh . . . well. I'd be a damn sight more pleased if you'd remember to do what I asked. [*Calming down*] What is this job, then?

COLETTE: I start work tomorrow at the leather factory.

MUM: How much?

COLETTE: Ninety dollars fifty a week. That's not bad, is it? And the work doesn't look too hard.

MUM: Well, that should suit you. You wouldn't know what hard work is. I do all the work around this place. You should try running this place for fifteen years. Cooking, cleaning, washing. Looking after you kids. Nobody pays me a red cent for all I do around here.

COLETTE: Yeah, well, you're a mum. That's your job. You're supposed to do it for love.

MUM: Love? Twenty-four hours a day every day of the year. I don't know about love. I think I was mad to get married at all.

COLETTE: Aw, change the record, Mum. At least ya can't say I'm bludging anymore.

MUM: Yeh, well, I must admit the money'll come in handy. I should go out to work. That's what I should do. Get myself a job.

COLETTE: What for? If you wait a bit longer you'll be getting the old age pension.

MUM: Don't be so damn cheeky.

COLETTE: Well, you're too old. I don't think married women should work. There'd be a lot more jobs for kids if they didn't.

MUM: And that's a load of bull. Who told you that?

COLETTE: It says it in the papers.

MUM: Well, that shows they don't know as much as they think they do. A lot of those women have been in work most of their life. You can't buy experience with money. You buy it with years.

COLETTE: How would you know? You haven't worked since I was born.

MUM: That's right. I don't work — I'm just married. [*She exits.*]

SCENE FOUR

The factory. VI *enters with the girls. They freeze. The machine sounds start. The girls work.* VI *changes the date to November and the time to ten. Siren. The girls start to move to the canteen.*

VI: Hang on, girls. Mr Naylor wants to have a word with us.

CONNIE: [*to* VI] What do you think that's about?

VI: New machines, I hope.

COLETTE: What about a dishwasher — I'm sick of washing up.

DI: I'd sooner have a raise.

CONNIE: Bet he's going to raise the quotas. Make us work harder.

DI: Can he do that?

VI: Not without union consent, he can't.
    [NAYLOR *enters.*]

NAYLOR: Good morning, ladies.

COLETTE: Morning, Mr Naylor.

OTHERS: Morning.

NAYLOR: I won't keep you long. I just want a few words with you . . . Well . . . I started this firm nine years ago. Vi was with me then and I think I can say that it's been a good place to work . . . for all of us . . . and what I have to say now is something I hoped I'd never have to say but . . .

CONNIE: Get on with it.

NAYLOR: I've just received word from the directors in Sydney that our factory is going to close down.

[*There is a general reaction.*]

DI: Close?

NAYLOR: I realise this will come as a bit of a shock to you.

CONNIE: Flaming earthquake.

NAYLOR: I had no idea myself.

CONNIE: Well, how long have we got, then?

NAYLOR: You'll all be retrenched from Friday next week.

COLETTE: Retrenched. Next week.

VI: But . . . it's only four weeks to Christmas. Will we get our Christmas bonus?

NAYLOR: I'm sorry, no.

CONNIE: Christ.

NAYLOR: The Board says you're not entitled.

CONNIE: And a Merry Christmas to them, too.

NAYLOR: The thing is we just can't compete with Asian imports any more. There's no other way out. Well, Vi, let the girls have an extra five minutes.

[NAYLOR *goes. The girls look at each other.*]

CONNIE: Five minutes? I'll need the three weeks to get over that shock.

COLETTE: Why does Mr Naylor have to close us down?

VI: It's not him. Naylor's only the manager. It's owned by this big firm in Sydney.

CONNIE: It wouldn't have happened if we'd got the new machines in. We'd have raised our quota and no worries.

VI: It's not that, Connie. We've been making money and the work was good. I know.

CONNIE: So, why are they closing us down? What more do they want? I gave blood last Saturday morning.

COLETTE: My mum's gonna kill me.

CONNIE: It's not your fault.

COLETTE: She told me. She said I wouldn't be able to keep this job.

CONNIE: It's the job that's not keeping you.

VI: How about you, Di? You don't get any maintenance.

DI: I'll have to look for another job.

CONNIE: You'll be lucky. At least I've got Bob working. Not

that he's going to be pleased about cutting back.

DI: I'd never manage on the pension. And Christmas? What about Christmas?

CONNIE: You can always tell the kids Santa Claus is dead. No bonus. That's a blow. [*To* DI] Hey, did Ted know anything about this before he went? Is that why he left?

DI: I'm sure he didn't. I don't think so.

VI: It's not right, you know. We've earned that bonus. They ought to keep us on, at least until Christmas. I mean, four more weeks? I'll tell you what. I've a good mind to get on to the union. Why not?

DI: Yeah, why not?

VI: They can negotiate with the firm. We've been making a profit. What would it cost them to keep the place open a few more weeks? It's Housing Trust property and subsidised rent. I'll get onto the union.

CONNIE: Make them work for their money for once. We pay enough out.

VI: We're entitled. Right. We'll bring in the union.
   [*They all freeze.*]

SCENE FIVE

CONNIE *and* BOB *are at one side of the stage;* VI *and* EDDIE *are at the other.* VI *and* EDDIE *freeze.*

CONNIE: Bob. Bob. Are you there? Bob.

BOB: In here, Connie. What's the matter now? Have we won the lottery?

CONNIE: Wish we had. You won't believe this. [*Kissing him*] The factory's closing down.

BOB: Your factory?

CONNIE: Yeah. I told you, you wouldn't believe it.

BOB: I believe it, but I don't like it. Why are they closing? I thought they were doing all right.

CONNIE: Well, Mr Naylor told us they're bringing in cheap goods from Asia. They just don't need us any more.

BOB: Hang on, you said the factory's closing down. You didn't say anything about you losing your job.

CONNIE: Well, without the factory working it follows that we won't be either.

BOB: But, you've always worked, Connie. Your money's helping us pay for the holiday at Christmas. They can't do that.

CONNIE: Well, they have, and that's that.

BOB: I suppose you lot just sat there and let him sack you? If that had happened down at the works we'd have had the union rep in like a shot. That's the trouble with you sheilas, you're not politically-minded enough.

[CONNIE *and* BOB *freeze*.]

EDDIE: You phoned the union rep? You're getting a bit political, aren't you?

VI: I've always been a bit political. I've just never got around to doing much about it.

EDDIE: I'm not knocking you, love, you know that.

VI: I know, Eddie. I suppose I'm a bit worked up about it all. The trouble with this country is they think women shouldn't work at all. Well, I've always worked, and me mum and me grandma. I mean, we took it for granted.

EDDIE: Course, my mum didn't go out to work, Vi.

VI: Yeah, well, she had eight kids, didn't she? But nobody thought they were doing you a favour if they gave you a job, did they? For God's sake, this is an industrial nation, not a cow paddock with lights. Look, we're all cogs in the work machine, right? So why put the cogs out in the field and let them go rusty? Women have just as much right to work as anybody else.

EDDIE: Yeah, well, that's the crunch, I suppose. It's easier to put women off when the going gets tough.

[VI *and* EDDIE *freeze*.]

CONNIE: It's going to be tough, Bob.

BOB: You're telling me. We'll never manage on just my wage. I'll be able to keep up the mortage and the car payments, the important things. But what about everything else you pay for?

CONNIE: The important things! My money is just as important as yours. I work hard for that money, Bob. They don't give it to me. Have you thought about the kids and their Christmas presents? Who's going to pay for them?

BOB: I dunno.

CONNIE: I promised myself they'd never go without. They've got as much right as any other kid and if I have to work to give it to them, well, I'm damn well going to.

> [CONNIE *and* BOB *freeze.*]

VI: It's not right, you know. Most of those girls have been working a long time. They're used to the money. And even the one's who haven't, like Colette . . . Where's Colette going to get another job? Eight weeks' experience? She'll probably end up getting married because she can't think of anything better to do.

EDDIE: [*protesting*] Here, Vi . . .

VI: I'm talking about getting married before you're ready for it. Couple of kids get married, then they have a couple of kids and then they both turn round and say, 'Here, hang on, what happened to my youth?'

EDDIE: So he goes looking for a bit of excitement.

VI: And she's left home wondering why women always get the rotten end of the stick. It's not good enough. We're entitled to our jobs and Colette's entitled to a better chance than she's getting.

> [VI *and* EDDIE *freeze.*]

CONNIE: We've got a better chance of surviving than some.

BOB: We'll just have to re-adjust, cut down.

CONNIE: Hmmm. What about Di, though? No husband and two kids. What's she going to do now she's unemployed?

BOB: Wait a minute, first things first. Di's OK, she can get the pension. But they won't even count you as unemployed. Let's worry about ourselves first, eh, love?

CONNIE: Yeah, I suppose you're right. I'll just put the snags on, eh, love?

> [*They all go off.*]

SCENE SIX

---

*The factory. The girls enter and freeze. The machine noise
starts and the women work.* VI *puts the time to three-forty-
five.*

VI: [*looking at her watch*] Righto, girls. We've got Mr
  Dougherty, the union rep, coming in a couple of minutes,
  so we'll stop now.
COLETTE: What can he do?
VI: Well, we'll see, won't we, when he comes in. He's our
  union secretary, the Australian Textile Workers, so he
  might be able to come up with something.
  [DOUGHERTY *enters.*]
  Mr Dougherty. . .
DOUGHERTY: Hello. Call me Reg.
VI: Oh, yes. Reg. I'm Vi Griffiths.
DOUGHERTY: How do you do.
VI: Girls, this is Mr Dougherty — Reg.
DOUGHERTY: All the girls here?
  [*There is a general murmur of assent.*]
  Good afternoon, girls. Well, I've been doing a bit of
  homework on your behalf. And I'm here now to see what I
  can do to sort this business out. [*To* VI] Right, now if you
  could repeat exactly what the management said to you on
  Friday, please, Vi.
COLETTE: He sacked us . . .
DOUGHERTY: Vi?
VI: Right, then. Mr Naylor came in and told us the factory
  was going to close down. Just like that.
  [*The girls murmur assent.*]
  And we were all to finish up on Friday.
CONNIE: No Christmas bonus either.
DOUGHERTY: That's not on, for a start. Now, what reasons
  did he give you?
VI: We can't compete with the goods coming in from
  overseas.

DOUGHERTY: That's all?

> [*There is a general hubbub.*]

Well, I'll tell you what we've found out. It's not that they *can't* compete, they don't *want* to compete with overseas imports.

VI: Hey? What do you mean, Reg?

DOUGHERTY: Where are these cheap goods coming from?

VI: Hong Kong.

DOUGHERTY: Guess who owns the factory in Hong Kong?

CONNIE: King Kong.

COLETTE: You mean Kung Fu.

VI: [*getting the message*] You mean . . . Shut up, girls, this is important.

DOUGHERTY: [*nodding*] Right. Protectaware.

VI: Well, the sneaky. . .

COLETTE: What? What's that he's saying, Vi?

VI: They're taking the work off us because they can do it cheaper in their Hong Kong factory.

DOUGHERTY: Now, how much an hour do you girls get paid?

CONNIE: Shouldn't he know that?

VI: About four dollars sixty an hour, graded down.

DOUGHERTY: Well, a worker in Hong Kong gets paid that for the whole week.

DI: What? That's terrible.

COLETTE: Jeez! How do they live?

CONNIE: Probably on rice power.

COLETTE: Shut up, Connie.

DOUGHERTY: So that's the situation. It's a question of economics.

VI: But we've been making a profit.

DOUGHERTY: Yes, but Protectaware get a bigger profit manufacturing in Hong Kong. So you girls get the chop.

DI: Disgusting.

DOUGHERTY: The union's right behind you. We're determined to fight this.

CONNIE: Good on you, Reg.

VI: So, what do you suggest we do?

DOUGHERTY: I suggest we take industrial action.

VI: Strike. We haven't got any jobs to start off with.

COLETTE: I don't think my dad would like it.

CONNIE: Shut up, Colette.

DOUGHERTY: No, not strike. I propose we stage a sit-in.
  [*There is a general murmur.*]

VI: [*to* DOUGHERTY] You mean, take over the factory?

DOUGHERTY: Yes, it'll attract the media. They'll be in here
  like blow-flies at a butchers' picnic.

COLETTE: What's the media?

VI: Newspapers, love.

DI: And telly . . .

COLETTE: Telly? Jeez.

CONNIE: I wonder if I'll have time to get my hair done?

DI: Cut it Chinese style and they might give you your job
  back.

COLETTE: Hey, how will them in Hong Kong know we're sitting down?

DOUGHERTY: Any serious questions?

VI: Hang on, that was a serious question.

DOUGHERTY: It's not the Hong Kong workers we're against,
  it's the bosses here.

VI: See, we've got to show them that they can't do this to us.

CONNIE: Yeah, up and at 'em.

DI: Those cheapies only last a few hours.

VI: So if we stage this sit-in, I reckon we'll draw quite a
  crowd.

CONNIE: What do we actually do, Reg?

DOUGHERTY: Just stay here for twenty-four hours a day.
  [*There is a general hubbub.*]
  There's no reason to upset your home lives. The other
  unions will support you on this. We'll organise a roster
  system. You do your normal hours, the men will do the
  night shift, and so on.

CONNIE: Ooh, I might do the night shift and so on myself.

DI: No hope of getting paid, I suppose?

DOUGHERTY: No. You won't get paid. But it's worth a try.
  At the very least, I guarantee you'll get your Christmas
  bonuses.

CONNIE: That would be worth it, wouldn't it?

VI: We've got nothing to lose.

COLETTE: 'Cept four days' pay.

CONNIE: Oh, come on, Colette. One in, all in. You're one of us now.

VI: Oh, just one thing, Reg. We won't be working the machines at all, will we?

DOUGHERTY: No. You won't be working. You just stay in the factory.

CONNIE: I might even finish knitting that jumper for Bob.

DI: You mean that grey one you started two years ago?

CONNIE: It was off-white when I started.

COLETTE: We can bring mags and stuff.

CONNIE: And my little telly. I can catch up on those serials I haven't seen for years.

DI: I could do with a bit of romance for a change.

VI: Right, what do you say, girls?

DOUGHERTY: Can we take a show of hands? All those in favour of occupying the Protectaware premises as from tomorrow morning, raise their right hand.

[*All do*]

Good. It's unanimous. [*To* VI] Right.

I've got to get busy. We have to have a good crowd outside when you arrive in the morning.

[DOUGHERTY *goes off.*]

VI: Yeah, no use hiding your light under a bushel. OK, girls. You'd better nick off now and get yourselves organised. See ya tomorrow, then. Bright and smiling for the telly.

[*The girls move off, talking excitedly.* VI *moves the clock to four and the siren sounds.*]

SCENE SEVEN

EDDIE: [*off*] Come on, Vi! Where are you?

VI: In here.

[EDDIE *enters.*]

EDDIE: Hurry up or we'll miss the bus.

VI: Never mind the bus. Hey, guess what. We're going to

have a sit-in.

EDDIE: You what?

VI: Dougherty reckons if we stage a sit-in, we'll get our bonus.

EDDIE: And what about the jobs?

VI: Couldn't promise anything there, but at least we'll get on the telly.

EDDIE: Telly?

VI: He's going to get them down here tomorrow. Them and all the other unions. I'll be on the News. Waving my banner, 'Women of the World Unite'.

EDDIE: Er, I don't know that I'm so keen on the telly, though.

VI: Why not? It'll be bad publicity for Protectaware.

EDDIE: It'll be bad publicity for me, and all.

VI: What d'you mean?

EDDIE: Up at the works.

VI: What're you on about?

EDDIE: My boss isn't going to like it, is he?

VI: What's it got to do with him?

EDDIE: He won't like seeing my wife red-ragging it on the telly. He's dead against commos.

VI: Commos, me? Give over.

EDDIE: You'll be rocking the boat, love. And if he reckons I'm behind you, he might think twice about keeping me on as foreman.

VI: Sack you? He couldn't do that, you've worked years to get that job.

EDDIE: That's what I mean. It's not worth mucking all that up over something you're going to lose, in any case, in four weeks.

VI: You reckon they're going to take that line on it?

EDDIE: Well, I think he would, love. Think about it.

VI: I don't like leaving the girls in the lurch.

EDDIE: You won't be leaving them in the lurch. They'll understand your position. You're twice as old as any of them. They'll understand that.

VI: It's just that — back home, me Dad was a union organiser. We've always stood behind.

EDDIE: Yeah, but you understand what I'm saying, don't you?

VI: You're right. Yeah.

[*They go off.*]

SCENE EIGHT

The Manders' family home. COLETTE *enters and sits watching television.*

MUM: [*off*] What about some help in the kitchen, Colette?

COLETTE: Aw, I'm watching TV.

MUM: [*off*] You're always watching TV. It's about time you did some work around the place.

COLETTE: I work.

[MUM *enters.*]

MUM: You go to that factory. Whether they get any work out of you is another matter. If you put as much energy into your work as you do watching that rubbish, you'd be running the place before you could turn around.

COLETTE: It won't matter after next week anyway.

MUM: Don't speak under your breath. If you've got something to say, you say it. But hurry up, I've got the griller on.

COLETTE: I'm trying to tell you. The factory is closing down.

MUM: What? So you've lost your job, have you?

COLETTE: I didn't lose the job.

MUM: Well, that's just wonderful. How am I going to pay off the new vacuum cleaner? It's your money paying for that, you know. Well, what happened then?

COLETTE: They just don't want the gloves or something.

MUM: Who doesn't want the gloves or something?

COLETTE: I don't know, none of the girls bloody know.

MUM: Don't swear at me, young lady. That'd be just like you, you wouldn't know what was going on if you fell over it.

COLETTE: I do know. This guy he came in today, the union

guy.

MUM: Huh, unions. Don't let your dad hear you talking about them.

COLETTE: And he said if we go into the factory tomorrow and lock the doors and stay there, we might get our jobs back.

MUM: What?

COLETTE: Yeah, we're gonna have a sit-down or something.

MUM: A sit-down? You mean a sit-in. Well, I might have guessed you'd finish up in a recumbent position.

COLETTE: Eh?

MUM: On your bum!

SCENE NINE

The factory. The siren sounds. The girls enter with general noise and laughter.

DI: Did you see that?

COLETTE: And they were punching each other. Jeez, look at those people. Hey, look, look at that.

DI: What's Mr Naylor doing?

CONNIE: Ooh, pushy. That was a bit rough, wasn't it?

COLETTE: Shove over, I can't see properly. Where's the telly? What's going on over there?

CONNIE: It's Naylor. He parted the crowd like Moses on the Red Sea. There he is. He's talking to a cop.

COLETTE: Where? Show me.

CONNIE: He's pointing at us.

DI: Yoohoo, Mr Naylor.

CONNIE: Di.

COLETTE: [*showing off*] Here. Watch this.

DI: He couldn't have seen you from there.

COLETTE: I know. I'm not dumb. Hey, do you think he's going to have us arrested?

CONNIE: No. No. Look, the fuzz is shaking his head.

COLETTE: My mother'll kill me if I get a record.

CONNIE: It's all right. He's getting into his car and driving away.

    [*All cheer.*]

DI: Bye-bye, Mr Naylor.

CONNIE: Didn't he look ropeable, though?

COLETTE: Nah. Nah. We won. We won.

CONNIE: We won the battle but the war's still on. Hey, look at those young union blokes. Ooh. They're looking at us.

DI: I like him.

COLETTE: Hey, you! My friend thinks you're sexy.

DI: Shut up, Colette.

CONNIE: Ooh, yes, he's got lovely eyes. [*Nudging* DI] How would you like his shoes under your bed?

    [*Shouting*] Have you come to sit with us?

COLETTE: Hey, spunky, come here and I'll hold your sign for you.

CONNIE: [*pretending*] Colette, isn't that your mother out there?

COLETTE: Where? She isn't!

DI: See that one with the striped jacket? I like him.

CONNIE: He looks like a mint humbug.

COLETTE: It's a pity Vi isn't here.

DI: Let's get organised.

CONNIE: I'll just blow my public a big kiss. Look at Dougherty's face. I don't think he liked that.

DI: I'm going to put my stuff here.

CONNIE: I'll have two chairs. One for my feet. This is what happens every time me and Bob have a row. He gets the bed and I get the chairs.

COLETTE: Where can I go?

DI: Ask a silly question.

COLETTE: Aw, you know what I mean. Hey, I know. I'll get the chair out of Mr Naylor's office.

DI: You can't do that...

CONNIE: It'll probably growl at you.

COLETTE: Right. I'm manager today.

CONNIE: How about that for a quick promotion?

COLETTE: That's enough chit-chat, Connie. If you didn't put in so much overtime with your mouth you might get your quotas out on time. I'd make a good manager, wouldn't I? I might apply for the job.

CONNIE: Get her. You're the wrong sex, love.

DI: What about a cup of tea?

COLETTE: It's not break time.

CONNIE: It's break time all day today. [*Sprawling out on the chairs*] Up the workers.

　　[*They freeze.* DI *changes the time to two thirty-five.*]

SCENE TEN

DOUGHERTY *moves to the box and stands on it. The girls change positions. They freeze.*

DI: An hour and twenty-five minutes to go.
　　[*Pause.*]
Wonder if the wives of the union blokes'll be angry, them sitting in here all night?

CONNIE: Nah, probably be glad of the rest.

DI: How come every conversation in this place comes back to S—E—X.

COLETTE: It's all right, you can say it. I know what it means.
　　[*They laugh and freeze.*]

REPORTER ONE: [*off*] Margaret Brien, ABC *P.M.* Mr Dougherty, exactly how many women are involved in the sit-in?

DOUGHERTY: There's twenty-five girls altogether.

REPORTER TWO: [*off*] Ralph O'Connell, D.N. *News.* And what are they doing in the factory?

DOUGHERTY: They're keeping themselves occupied.

REPORTER TWO: [*off*] Are they actually working?

DOUGHERTY: Not on the machines, they're not. They're busy gathering support right around the country, writing letters to Members of Parliament and so on.

REPORTER ONE: [*off*] What do they hope to gain by this action?

DOUGHERTY: Exactly what's happening: to make people

stand up and take notice of these firms ripping off Australian jobs?

[DOUGHERTY *freezes. The girls change positions.*]

COLETTE: Hey, you know, if Mr Naylor'd sell me the leather, youse guys could show me how to use the machines and then I can make up the gloves myself.

CONNIE: What for?

COLETTE: Something to do.

[*Pause.*]

CONNIE: Thought I might make Bob a bit of a stew tonight. — What do you reckon?

[*Pause.*]

DI: Thought I'd do crumbed snags.

[*Pause.*]

COLETTE: And then we could sell them at the craft market.

DI: Crumbed snags?

COLETTE: Nah, the gloves.

[*Pause.*]

CONNIE: Who's going to buy industrial gloves at a craft market?

[*They freeze.*]

REPORTER THREE: [*off*] Joan Hunter, AAP. What's the situation now, Mr Dougherty?

DOUGHERTY: How do you mean, love?

REPORTER THREE: [*off*] I mean, Mr Dougherty, has the firm given any ground at all or are these women wasting their time?

DOUGHERTY: The union is not only negotiating with the firm but also with the State Government, who are taking a close interest in this matter.

REPORTER THREE: [*off*] Can you give us any details, then?

DOUGHERTY: I've got another meeting with the Minister and representatives of the firm tomorrow afternoon and that's all I can tell you at this stage.

REPORTER FOUR: [*off*] Mark Kelly, *News*. Mr Dougherty, what is the attitude of the husbands to all this?

DOUGHERTY: Total support.

[DOUGHERTY *freezes. The girls change positions.*]

DI: Cup of tea?

CONNIE: If I see another cup of tea I'll be sitting on the loo all night. Look like a cup of tea soon.

DI: And I'll go round the bend if I don't find some work to do soon.

CONNIE: Why don't you catch up on some sewing or something?

DI: No, I mean work. I don't know why we don't take up some of those offers that have been coming in. At least we'd be doing something.

CONNIE: Oh, I don't know, Di. Mr Dougherty said we weren't to touch the machines.

DI: Seems such a waste, sitting here for three days.

[*The telephone rings.* DI *lifts the receiver. All freeze.*]

REPORTERS: [*off*] What's the court's attitude? After three days, Mr Dougherty, how's morale? Protectaware's given in, is that true? When will we get some answers?

DOUGHERTY: Just hold your horses. I have a statement on behalf of the State Government, Protectaware and the union. The South Australian Government has decided to award a special contract to Protectaware and the firm has agreed to abide by the conditions of this contract which are as follows. One: the factory will remain in operation until Christmas. Two: all the women in Protectaware's employ will retain their jobs for this period, and Three: all the women in Protectaware's employ will receive their normal Christmas bonus.

REPORTER ONE: [*off*] Margaret Brian, ABC. Mr Dougherty, what about after Christmas?

DOUGHERTY: It's far too early to say yet, but certain proposals are being considered. You'll be informed if and when any of these eventuate.

[DOUGHERTY *freezes.*]

SCENE ELEVEN

DI: We've won!

[VI *enters with a cake tin.*]

COLETTE: We've won.

CONNIE: We've got work till Christmas.

DI: And our Christmas bonuses.

VI: Oh, that's wonderful.

COLETTE: And what about all those people ringing in.

CONNIE: Everyone's right behind us.

DI: We even get paid this week.

CONNIE: Oh . . . I don't know about you, Vi.

VI: Shouldn't think so.

CONNIE: First time I've been paid for sitting on my bum.

VI: Fancy Protectaware paying you.

CONNIE: They're trying to save face.

VI: And they're going to find us work until Christmas?

DI: No. We've got a Government contract to see us through.

VI: And after Christmas?

    [*There is a general hubbub.* VI *covers her ears.*]
One at a time.

CONNIE: You tell her, Colette. Ooh, you'll like this, Vi.

COLETTE: Reg Dougherty reckons we could run the place
ourselves.

VI: Us? Run the factory?

CONNIE: That's right.

DI: Like — who was it? Yeh, like Safcol.

VI: Oh, you mean like a co-op.

CONNIE: That's the word.

COLETTE: That's what he said. A women workers' co-op.

VI: That's marvellous. Come on, down to the pub, I'll treat
you to a drink.

    [*They all go off.*]

SCENE TWELVE

The Manders' home. COLETTE *is waiting.* MUM MANDERS
enters with a shopping bag.

COLETTE: Hey Mum, I own a factory!

MUM: God help Australia. . . You haven't started smoking

those funny cigarettes, have you?

COLETTE: Mum. No, just a few drinks. Mr Dougherty came in today and said it's all right with everyone if we form a co-op.

MUM: What co-op?

COLETTE: I told you about it before.

MUM: You mean you're actually going to run the factory yourselves?

COLETTE: Yup. We get to do everything, like tendering for orders and all that and this is the best part — we won't have no boss looking over our shoulders.

MUM: How are you going to organise yourselves without a boss?

COLETTE: Because it's ours. That means we'll work harder.

MUM: But who's going to do all the office work?

COLETTE: Mr Dougherty said we get to appoint a manager to do all that stuff but he isn't our boss. Not like Mr Naylor was because it's a co-op and that means we're all the same.

MUM: Well, I could be your manager.

COLETTE: What do you mean?

MUM: I've been managing you and this house for long enough. I can't see much difference.

COLETTE: Oh, don't be stupid, Mum. Vi's going to be the manager. It's just about definite.

MUM: Yeah, well, don't think I couldn't do it, 'cos I could.
  [*They go out.*]

SCENE THIRTEEN

The factory. VI *enters with the girls. The machine noise starts and the girls work.* VI *changes the sign to 'Working Women's Co-op' and the date to March.*

VI: [*to* COLETTE] Ready then?
  [COLETTE *goes into the office after* VI.]
CONNIE: Off for her managerial class.

VI: We'll have a look at the orders this morning. Now, when they come in, the office types copies. One goes to the buyer, that confirms it, and we keep the others. Pink and blue flimsies here.

COLETTE: Right. A lot of paper work, huh?

VI: Yeah, I sometimes think we process more paper than we do gloves.

[TED *enters and goes to his office, frowning to see* VI *and* COLETTE *at his desk.*]

TED: Hello, hello, hello, what have we here?

VI: It's all right, Ted. I'm just showing Colette how the order system works.

COLETTE: It's sort of more interesting when you know who's getting the gloves.

TED: Well, I've got phone calls to make.

COLETTE: We won't be long. I've got to get back soon, I'll be behind.

VI: Can't you find something to do on the floor?

COLETTE: It needs sweeping for a start.

[VI *shakes her head at* COLETTE. TED *looks annoyed, but tries to hold it down.*]

TED: You could do that in the tea room.

VI: Oh, Ted, you don't run a factory from the tea room.

TED: But this is my office.

COLETTE: And it's our factory.

[VI *laughs.*]

TED: Well, since you're the boss, I'll let you. [*To* COLETTE] I had to work my way up to that sort of job.

COLETTE: Yeah, well, I decided to start at the top.

[TED *stands undecidedly.*]

VI: It's OK, Ted, [*Dismissing him*] We won't be a minute.

COLETTE: See you later, Ted.

[TED *grunts and goes back to the factory floor. He fiddles with a machine and gets his hands dirty. He looks for a piece of rag to wipe them with.* COLETTE *looks out after him.*]

Creep.

VI: OK, Colette.

COLETTE: Why did they make him manager? It should have

been you.

VI: I didn't get the votes, did I?

COLETTE: Plenty of them wanted you. It was Di . . .

VI: Look, some women just don't like being bossed around by another woman. But they all like being told what to do.

COLETTE: Stupid. Fancy voting for Ted Spence.

VI: Well, it's done now. I wasn't going to push it. Me not being in the sit-in, and being a lot older, it might've looked like I was trying to pull weight.

[*They bend over the files again.*]

TED: How's this batch going?

CONNIE: Great. Nearly through this lot already.

DI: What happened to Colette? She's not slacking off, is she?

[TED *looks back towards the office.*]

TED: [*peevishly*] In the office. Playing with the filing system.

CONNIE: She can be your secretary.

TED: That'll be the day.

CONNIE: She reckons she's good at maths.

DI: [*acidly*] She can't spell.

CONNIE: Who can? I reckon we all ought to have a go at it.

DI: Hey, Ted, what's after these aprons?

TED: Haven't you checked the orders? You're supposed to know about those things now you're the bosses.

CONNIE: We don't want to be bothered with all that. We just want to get on with our work. You do that. That's what you're paid for.

TED: How can I do it if I can't even get into my own office? You pay me to be the manager.

CONNIE: That's right. When are you going to manage to look at this machine for me?

TED: It's still playing up?

CONNIE: Not the only thing.

DI: You'll have your office back in a minute, Ted.

TED: I'm just trying to make my position clear . . .

CONNIE: Put a sock in it, will you, Ted. We want to finish this batch.

DI: I'm ahead of you now, Connie.

CONNIE: It's this rotten machine. All right, Di, you're on.

Watch my dust.

> [CONNIE *speeds up.* TED *looks at his watch and wanders towards the office, hesitates and wanders back to* DI.]

TED: [*muttering*] Just keep your eye on Colette, will you. She's getting too damn cheeky.

DI: Me? I'm just one of your bosses, love.

TED: I thought you were on my side.

CONNIE: [*shouting*] No bludging, Di. Get your head down.

DI: We're all in this together, Ted.

TED: But I thought you could, well . . .

DI: Nothing doing, Ted. Sorry.

> [TED *looks at her and then walks away. She shrugs and puts her head down to work.*]

COLETTE: You know what day it is today?

VI: Friday.

COLETTE: Pay day.

VI: Used to be pay day.

COLETTE: I'd started getting used to having money.

VI: You're an executive now, love. You'll have to live on credit.

COLETTE: Hey, imagine me walking into Myers saying 'Charge it to the firm.'

VI: Don't you dare, madam.

COLETTE: Only kidding.

VI: Come on. We won't get any money till we get these orders out.

> [TED *watches the girls working.*]

TED: [*to* DI] How're you going?

DI: Be finished by lunchtime, I reckon. We're beating the quota.

TED: Something to celebrate.

CONNIE: You could take us to the pub in your company car.

TED: I can't do that, Connie. I'm only given that car for business purposes. How would it look if . . .

DI: Oh. She's having a joke, Ted.

> [COLETTE *comes down from the office.*]

CONNIE: Here she comes. Miss Big. Today the factory, tomorrow the world.

COLETTE: Don't let Vi hear youse. She wants us all to learn about pink and blue flimsies.

CONNIE: Oh. How boring.

COLETTE: [*seeing the pile of finished work*] Jeez, you've done all that already. I'll never catch up.

[COLETTE *sits at her machine.* VI *and* TED *walk back to office.*]

TED: Somebody ought to do something about that kid.

VI: Ah. You can't expect any more off her at this stage.

[VI *changes the time to ten. The siren sounds for tea break.*]

CONNIE: Damn. I haven't finished.

DI: Only five more to go.

CONNIE: We'll carry on, hey Di?

DI: Yeah. I'm mad, unpaid work and no tea break.

CONNIE: We'll get paid, right? A nice lump sum, I hope. Hey, Colette. Can you get Vera out of the loo? You don't take ten minutes for nature calls when you're working for yourself.

COLETTE: Vera, you can come out now, it's tea break.

DI: What are you going to spend all your hard-earned wealth on, Connie?

CONNIE: I shall just throw it on top of the wardrobe and let it breed.

DI: I'll bet. I'll buy a nice picture, something good to look at instead of your back.

CONNIE: What about Sinatra?

COLETTE: But he's old.

CONNIE: He's still sexy.

COLETTE: And we could get air-conditioning in.

CONNIE: Don't go overboard, Colette, we haven't got it yet. Two more to go.

VI: Working through their tea breaks? Wonders never cease.

TED: As long as they don't complain about it later. I'm damned if I'll work through my tea break.

VI: [*dryly*] You're entitled, you're the only one getting a regular wage.

DI: Done.

CONNIE: Yippee. Protectaware look out.

COLETTE: Wow. [COLETTE *works on.*]
TED: What's all the racket about?
CONNIE: We've finished the batch in record time.
TED: Well, I think this calls for a little celebration.
     [*He takes out bottles of Starwine.* TED *and* VI *go to the factory floor.* TED *holds the Starwine behind his back and then produces it with a flourish.*]
   Didn't let you down, did I?
ALL: Oh, Ted!
     [*All freeze. The women exit.*]

SCENE FOURTEEN

The machines start. TED *moves the date to June.* DOUGHERTY *comes in.*

TED: Come in, Reg. What have you got for us?
DOUGHERTY: This is from the meatworks. They seem happy.
TED: So they should be — the girls had the order out within a week. No news on that cheque from the cold-store contract, yet?
DOUGHERTY: I rang them again yesterday. They said they'd get straight onto it.
TED: I wish they'd hurry up. Things are getting pretty tight for the girls, waiting for their money.
DOUGHERTY: How's the work going?
TED: Good. Since they started the co-op, I've never seen them work so hard.
DOUGHERTY: Only natural, I suppose. Bit of incentive. Hope it doesn't turn them all into raging capitalists.
TED: Yeah, I'll give it to them, they can work. But they'd never make execs. They're happy so long as the orders keep coming.
DOUGHERTY: How about this one, then. They're doing a bit of renovation on the dining room of the Trades Hall. I reckon I could get you a bulk order for their red

  tablecloths.

TED: Mmmm. Red tablecloths. Sounds all right, though.

DOUGHERTY: You never know. Red today — white for the Lord Mayor's banquet tomorrow.

TED: Suits me. Get into some quality goods. Stop them dropping hints about me giving up the work car. . .

  [*He laughs.*]

DOUGHERTY: Commodore, isn't it?

TED: You need a decent car if you're trying to put over a good image.

DOUGHERTY: Wanted you to go in for a smaller one, did they?

TED: Suggested I use my own and draw expenses. 'Course, they were only joking.

DOUGHERTY: It's a point. They'll have to learn to cut corners if they want to get this thing off the ground. It might be a good idea to take it seriously.

TED: Oh, do you think so?

DOUGHERTY: Well, it's up to them, of course. They're the bosses. Why don't you take it to the girls and discuss it?

TED: Yeah, OK. Good idea.

DOUGHERTY: Hell! I've got to go. Let me know what they decide.

TED: About the tablecloths?

DOUGHERTY: And the car.

  [TED *moves the clock to twelve-thirty.* DOUGHERTY *leaves.*]

SCENE FIFTEEN

DI *enters.*

TED: There's something you could do for me.

DI: Sure, love.

TED: It's about Colette.

DI: Colette?

TED: She's too slow on the line and she's getting too big for her boots.

DI: So?

TED: So, I suggest she's given her notice.

DI: What are you telling me for?

TED: Because you lot won't give me the right to hire and fire. She's got to go. And you've got to push it with the other girls.

DI: No. I wouldn't like to do that, Ted. It doesn't seem right.

TED: Come on. You girls won't allow me to do it. So you've got to.

DI: No.

[*The other women enter.* TED *brushes past them angrily.*]

CONNIE: What's up with Ted, then? Don't tell me Lois Lane knocked back Superman for once!

VI: Everybody ready, then?

COLETTE: What for?

DI: Ted's meeting.

CONNIE: Not another one.

VI: Aren't you coming then?

COLETTE: Do we have to?

VI: Well, I suppose not. But it is a co-op. It's best if everybody is there.

COLETTE: Yeah, I know that. But I'm miles behind with the quota.

[VI *and* DI *look up.*]

VI: Well, it's up to you.

COLETTE: Oh, all right, then.

CONNIE: Well, I'm fixing my machine.

[TED *enters from the office.*]

TED: Is this all that's coming?

VI: Yeah. About half. They're not very organisation-minded.

DI: Well, what have you got for us, Ted?

TED: You'll be pleased to hear Reg Dougherty dropped by with another cheque.

DI: Oh, great.

TED: It's not a lot, mind you.

VI: Every little counts. What else did he say?

DI: Any more contracts?

TED: Just a suggestion. He wants to know if we could handle a large order for red tablecloths.

DI: Those machines are for leather. Remember we tried that sample for the gym tunics.

VI: And there was Colette's dress.

COLETTE: [*laughing*] Yeah.

VI: It's a pity. Those Hong Kong factories still get most of the leather orders. We could do with some other lines as well.

TED: The tablecloth idea was the only one he came up with, I'm afraid.

VI: That's no good. These orders aren't going to last for ever.

DI: We'll have to start selling the furniture and things to make ends meet.

COLETTE: Isn't that what we said before... [*looking at* TED] About Ted's car?

TED: [*hastily*] What about cutting back on employees?

VI: What are you talking about, Ted? I thought the whole object of the exercise was jobs for the girls.

TED: We could cut away some of the dead wood.

VI: What dead wood?

TED: There's Vera, for instance.

COLETTE: What about Vera?

TED: She takes too many breaks. Anybody who has to go to the loo as often as Vera does should get a job as a lavatory cleaner.

COLETTE: She only goes because she's got a weak stomach and you give her the...

    [*Laughter.*]

TED: Look, this is no way to run a factory!

VI: Well, it's being run twice as well as when Protectaware were in, and we're getting more work out.

DI: We're only being held back by those ancient machines, Ted.

VI: My Eddie was saying last night we should get a loan from the bank to buy new ones.

DI: Could we do that?

VI: Why not? We've proved the co-op works. We'd be a good investment. I wouldn't mind having a go at them. What do you say, Ted? You and me could go and talk to the banks.

TED: I suppose so.

VI: Right. You're on. What else did he say?

TED: Nothing. That was all.

COLETTE: Hey, why didn't he come to the meeting? I thought he was supposed to be helping us!

TED: There's no point, is there? It's easier if he tells me; then I can explain it to you. Anyway, we don't want it to look as though the union is running us, do we?

DI: We don't have to worry. Ted'll look after things for us.

TED: Trust me.

SCENE SIXTEEN

TED *moves the date to July. The machines sound and the women work. They freeze.* TED *moves the date slowly from July to September. The machine noise slows down as September is reached and then dies. The women sit idle. They freeze.* VI *goes off.* REG DOUGHERTY *enters.*

DOUGHERTY: G'day, Ted.

TED: G'day, Reg. Have a seat.

DOUGHERTY: Here's the cheque for the foundry aprons and . . . you'll never guess what's in the post for you Monday.

TED: Don't tell me, the cheque for the cold-store contract?

DOUGHERTY: I put a bit of pressure on the. . .

TED: Thanks, Reg.

DOUGHERTY: Any new orders come through?

TED: Well, none that our machines can handle. Vi and I even tried going to the bank to borrow money for new machines.

DOUGHERTY: And?

TED: No go. Not enough security.

DOUGHERTY: Well, I might be onto something. There's

nothing definite at the moment. But I'm seeing a bloke tomorrow who's got a big jeans contract. Apparently what he usually does to guarantee quality is to lease the machines along with the job. Now, I reckon there'd still be a healthy profit in it for the co-op.

TED: Lease? We never thought of that.

DOUGHERTY: As I say, it's not definite but it sounds pretty promising.

TED: When can you let us know, Reg? Because we've really floundering at the moment.

DOUGHERTY: I'll be coming by this way on Monday. I'll drop in and let you know then.

TED: Thanks, Reg.

DOUGHERTY: Well . . . I see you've managed to hang onto the Commodore.

TED: Yeah, well, what with one thing and another, it just didn't come up.

DOUGHERTY: I'll see you Monday.

TED: OK, Reg.

[DOUGHERTY *goes off, followed by* TED.]

SCENE SEVENTEEN

The girls are hanging around trying to make work. DI *is sweeping up.* COLETTE *is reading a magazine in the canteen.*

DI: Move your feet.

CONNIE: There's nothing under my feet.

DI: I wanna finish the floor.

CONNIE: It's as clean as it'll get.

DI: You don't have to shout.

CONNIE: I'm not shouting.

DI: You were.

COLETTE: Shut up, will youse.

CONNIE: Eh?

COLETTE: You should hear yourselves.

CONNIE: Who asked your opinion?

COLETTE: Oh, God, you sound just like my mum.

CONNIE: I'll be just like your mum soon, stuck at home and with no work to do.

DI: I'm not worried about the work. It's the money not coming in.

CONNIE: Hey, Di, who was that man Ted was showing around the factory this morning?

DI: I think his name was Matheson.

CONNIE: Oh. Do you know if he's got any orders for us?

DI: I don't know. Ted doesn't tell me everything, you know.

CONNIE: Oh, pardon me. Hey, Colette, do you know who that man was?

COLETTE: I don't know. Hey, Di, there's a job here for you. 'Widowed man, fifty-five, two children, seeks companion/housekeep. Children no ob.'

CONNIE: Sounds all right. Might move in myself.

DI: Got enough trouble with two kids, let alone four and a man. Can I have a look?

COLETTE: Wouldn't bother. There's no factory work at all.

CONNIE: What are you going to do, Di?

[TED *enters with* VI.]

About time, Ted. We've been waiting for hours. Well, what have you got for us?

TED: Nothing definite.

CONNIE: Ah Christ! If you say that one more time, Ted, I'll . . .

TED: Keep your hair on, Connie. If you'd give us half a chance, I'd be able to explain what I've got for you. Call the girls for the meeting, Vi.

COLETTE: Not another one.

CONNIE: If you've got something to say, you can say it here.

VI: I suppose that's all right, Ted. Come on girls, it's worth it.

DI: May as well listen. Nothing else to do.

[VI *and* DI *get chairs for the meeting.*]

TED: I've got your money. And Reg and I are looking into a new large order.

COLETTE: Unreal. Great.

TED: Hang on, hang on. He didn't promise anything definite. It involves leasing suitable machines.

CONNIE: Yeah. We'll be making the royal wedding dress next.

TED: There's no need for that, Connie. I've been doing my best.

CONNIE: Yeah, you're a real ball of fire, Ted.

TED: Look, I'm getting a bit jack of getting rubbished every time things are a bit slack around here. It's about time you started treating me with a bit more respect.

CONNIE: I'll kiss your hand if you get us some orders quick smart.

TED: That's it, sit on your bum, dish out the orders and wait around until I get you work. If you listened for once instead of worrying about playing the part of a big executive, you'd have heard I could have some more work.

CONNIE: Oh, terrific. About time.

TED: Just let me do what I feel is in the best interests of your co-op. It'd make my job a lot easier.

VI: Now come on you two, enough arguing. Ted, love, do us a favour, give us the money and get to that leasing business. It's important. Could be just what we need to get us on our feet.

    [TED *goes into the office, freezes.* VI *and the girls go to the canteen.*]

CONNIE: Come on, girls, line up for your millions.

VI: Right. Here's the account book, kiddo. Let's get our economic situation organised.

    [*All freeze.*]

SCENE EIGHTEEN

DOUGHERTY: [*off*] Ted! Ted!

    [DOUGHERTY *enters. The girls remain frozen.*]

Ted. Look, I've only got a minute. Here's the number of that jeans bloke. He wants you to ring him straight away.

It's all set to go. This could be the saviour of the co-op.

TED: All our Christmases have come at once.

DOUGHERTY: Eh?

TED: I've had this man Matheson from Sydney looking around the factory all morning. He wants to buy the co-op out. Lock, stock and barrel.

DOUGHERTY: He what?

TED: He wants to buy the co-op. He's got factories in Sydney and Melbourne and he wants to set up here.

DOUGHERTY: But you don't need to sell now. That contract is just the beginning. There's at least six months' work there and once your name is known around the clothing manufacturers, you'll get heaps of work.

TED: I wouldn't be so quick to dismiss this other offer though, Reg.

DOUGHERTY: OK, look, what's the deal?

TED: He'll refit the factory with new machines, ones suitable for clothing. All the girls will keep their jobs. And they'll even be paid what the co-op owes them. It's a godsend, mate.

DOUGHERTY: What's in it for you?

TED: Well, I have the option of staying on as manager.

DOUGHERTY: It just seems a pity to let the co-op fold. What do the girls think?

TED: They don't know about it yet. I've called a meeting after lunch.

DOUGHERTY: I wish I could stay for it but I just can't. All you can do is put both offers to them and see which they want.

TED: Well, Reg, we both know it's their decision.

DOUGHERTY: Ring me tonight, will you, and let me know what they say?

TED: OK, Reg.

    [DOUGHERTY *goes out.*]

SCENE NINETEEN

The girls unfreeze. All look at TED.

VI: Oh Ted... We'll have to sell your car.
  [TED *looks at them and makes his decision.*]
TED: I've got a proposition for you. That man Matheson
  wants to buy the co-op out. We'll all keep our jobs, get
  back pay, new machines, and regular wages. What do you
  say?
  [*Pause. All raise their hands.*]

SCENE TWENTY

TED *changes the sign to 'Matheson Clothing Company'. The
girls all work as in Scene Two.*

VI: Oh, Ted ...
TED: Call me Mr Spence.
  [*All freeze.* TED *takes out a card.*]
Vi was moved onto the heavy presses. She retired two days
later.
  [*He hands* VI *her card; she exits.* TED *takes out another
  card.*]
Connie Dyer, declared redundant.
  [CONNIE *takes her card and exits.* TED *takes out
  another card.*]
Di was transferred to another Matheson factory.
  [*He hands* DI *her card.*]
Colette was replaced by another junior trainee. After six
months all the girls involved in the co-op had been re-
placed.

THE END